21 DAYS OF EVANGELISM
SMALL TASKS FOR GREAT COMMISSION OBEDIENCE

Alicia Tubbs

The Sudden Homesteader
JESUS LAND LOVE

21 DAYS OF EVANGELISM:
Small Tasks for Great Commission Obedience

Copyright © 2024 Alicia Tubbs
All rights reserved. No part of this publication may be reproduced or copied in any form without the written permission of the copyright owner.

Library of Congress Control Number: 2024906083

ISBN: 979-8-9858359-2-2

The Sudden Homesteader
Barnesville, GA
www.evangelizegeorgia.coms

Unless otherwise noted, scripture quotations taken from the (NASB®) New American Standard Bible®, Copyright © 1960, 1971, 1977, 1995 by The Lockman Foundation. Used by permission. All rights reserved. lockman.org

All Materials that accompany this book can be found on the *EVANGELIZE GEORGIA* website:

https://evangelizegeorgia.org/21-days-of-evangelism-book-free-materials/

Scan code for easy access to materials & FREE PDF of the book.

DO NOT PRINT THE PDF!
THE ONLINE PDF IS FOR READING ONLY!

Online Materials Include
- A free PDF File of this book
- "Free Gift" Gospel Tract
- Bible Verses for People Trapped in False Beliefs
- "FREE PRAYER" sign
- Link to Evangelism Crash Course (4 videos, 87 minutes total)
- Handout that accompanies Crash Course videos

Free Guides For Prayer and Fasting
Videos and handouts: https://evangelizegeorgia.org/free-guide-to-fasting/

21 DAYS OF EVANGELISM

CONTENTS

Acknowledgments

Disclaimer
Introductory Notes

1	The Forgotten Basics of Evangelism	9
2	Helpful Charts	39
3	Prepare Yourself For Evangelism	48
4	Put on the Full Armor of GOD	64
5	Prepare Your Materials for Evangelism	78

21 Evangelism Assignments (DAYS 1-21)   85-122
DAY 1 – Stand for JESUS.
DAY 2 – Thinking of You
DAY 3 – Be a Billboard for JESUS.
DAY 4 – Prayer Walk or Drive
DAY 5 – Front Lawn Evangelism
DAY 6 – Buy Giveaway Bibles.
DAY 7 – Bless People With Bibles.
DAY 8 – Brainstorm Your Tract.
DAY 9 – Draft Your Tract.
DAY 10 – Make Your Tract Eye-catching.
DAY 11 – Plan a Visit and Prepare a Gift.
DAY 12 – Practice to Proclaim.
DAY 13 – Edit and Print Your Tract.
DAY 14 – Bless Your Neighbor With a Visit.
DAY 15 – Prayer Walk or Drive Among the Poor
DAY 16 – Make a Blessing Bag.
DAY 17 – Give Away Your Blessing Bag.
DAY 18 – More Tracts!
DAY 19 – Bless Three Strangers.
DAY 20 – Print Your Sign and Pray.
DAY 21 – Evangelize in Public.

My Parting Words to You

> **Therefore everyone who hears these words of Mine and acts on them, may be compared to a wise man who built his house on the rock." -Matthew 7:24**

✝

The reason you're not evangelizing
isn't a lack of training.
It's a lack of obedience.

✝

If you're not proclaiming the cross of JESUS,
your church is a club,
your worship is entertainment,
your sermon is a lecture,
your Sunday school class is a social hour,
your home fellowship is a dinner party,
your children's ministry is childcare,
your outreach is social work,
your missions trip is a working vacation,
and your evangelism is small talk.

ACKNOWLEDGMENTS

Thank you FATHER in Heaven for creating me and sending JESUS to die for my sins. Thank you JESUS for willingly shedding your blood on the cross so I could have a way back to the FATHER.

Thank you to my husband for holding down the fort while I write, for providing for our family, for giving me the honest feedback I need, and for laying down his life for me as CHRIST laid down HIS life for the church.

Thanks to my children for playing outside when Mommy needed a quiet house.

Thanks, Dad, for being my first reader and Mom for being my first everything in life.

Thank you to my Dear Brothers and Sisters at the Prayer Tent and for my Beloved Church Family. Thank you to all the saints who follow me and support me online. Your prayers are more precious than gold. I look forward to the day when JESUS catches us up, and we can all fellowship face-to-face—forever.

Thanks to the many watchmen and women on *YouTube* and the Bible teachers who have remained true to a literal reading of OUR FATHER's word. I have learned so much over the years from your selfless efforts. I pray this book helps others to be edified in CHRIST JESUS OUR LORD. Anything good and helpful within these pages is from the HOLY SPIRIT. Anything else, including the typos, are from me.

DISCLAIMER

Please use wisdom and best practices when engaging in evangelism or leading others in the assignments in this book. It's best to avoid going anywhere in the dark, and it's good to have at least one other person with you at all times. You may have to evangelize alone at times. Please be safe. Know your rights and DO NOT FEAR.

Children and youth should never be left unattended when assisting adults with evangelistic tasks. Always be aware of physical dangers, such as lightning, and dogs.

Be informed: If you read this book, you are more accountable to take action than if you hadn't read it. GOD commands us to be doers of the word, not just hearers. If you hear about evangelism, you're expected to do evangelism. If you close this book and do nothing, you're like the foolish man who built his house on the sand.

Regarding fasting, please consult your doctor prior to beginning any type of food fast. This is especially important if you have a physical condition that is affected by your food intake, if you have any type of chronic illness, or are taking any kind of prescription medications. Please stop fasting if you feel ill, and seek medical attention if necessary. Please consult your doctor if you have any health concerns. Children and pregnant and nursing women should not fast from food.

INTRODUCTORY NOTES

Make Sure You're Going to Heaven.

Before proceeding in this book, or any other, take a moment to make sure you know where you're headed when this life is over. Even if you think you're saved, what's the harm in hearing the Gospel again? It can only strengthen your evangelism.

Also, there's always the chance you're self-deceived into thinking you're good with GOD. Many people I meet think they're going to Heaven and have even been baptized. Most of these people, however, cannot explain what it means to be saved, or they are completely misinformed about how a person becomes a child of GOD. Please take a moment to make sure you're not in this category of people.

Eternity is infinitely longer than this life, and everyone will spend eternity in either one of two places—paradise with GOD or Hell where the inhabitants are tormented in the Lake of Fire along with Satan and the demons. You can afford to make sure your eternal destiny is secure in JESUS.

To Get to Heaven, Believe the Gospel of JESUS CHRIST. All humans have two problems. We have all sinned and, as a consequence, our bodies will die someday. Worse still, because of our sin, we can't dwell with our perfect and holy GOD and are, therefore, destined to eternal death in the Lake of Fire.

Sin is anything from thinking bad thoughts about others, withholding forgiveness, having crushes on people to whom we're not married, speaking perversely, joking crudely, looking at bad things on the internet and other places, fornicating, cursing, misusing the names GOD and JESUS, getting drunk, abusing substances, indulging fantastical thoughts and desires, looking down on others, burdening others by being lazy or doing poor or incomplete work, neglecting family duties and employment obligations, incurring irresponsible debt, over-indulging in life's pleasures, being prideful or thinking we deserve a higher position, practicing gluttony, being greedy or stingy, wanting what others have, complaining about our lives, taking advantage of others, disrespecting or mocking our parents and those in authority over us, lying, stealing, cheating, bragging, slandering, gossiping, exaggerating to make ourselves look good, using company or church resources or time for personal projects or entertainment, putting our needs and preferences ahead of others, abusing our authority to get ahead or avoid consequences, offering or accepting bribes, living like the rules don't apply to us…The list goes on.

We're all guilty of at least one thing on this list. GOD is perfect and holy, and HE hates any sin of any kind. We will all eventually die as a result of our sins, and GOD also hates death. HE is the creator of life. GOD can't accept us as HIS children unless we are free of both sin and death.

We cannot take away our own sins. No human can forgive our sins. Our good deeds will never outweigh our bad ones. Being kind is good, but kindness can't pay for sin or make our bodies free of death. Being a good person can never make you a new person. Nothing on Earth can take away our sins and make our bodies immortal. If we're going to enter Heaven, where there is no sin and death, we need GOD HIMSELF to take away our sin and recreate our bodies without death. We need the CREATOR to recreate us.

God sent HIS SON JESUS down to Earth to do just that. JESUS was born into a flesh body. JESUS is GOD IN FLESH, THE MESSIAH. HE never sinned once during HIS life, and HE willingly died on the cross as the perfect LAMB OF GOD. Only JESUS is qualified to take away our sins because HE had no sin. No other sacrifice would satisfy the sin-debt that each person owes GOD. Only the perfect blood of the SON OF GOD is a high enough price to purchase a human soul from death to life.

After JESUS died, HE was buried and rose from the dead three days later into a body that will never die. Anyone who trusts in JESUS' death, burial, and resurrection to free us from sin and death, receives eternal life with GOD. The believer is reborn of the HOLY SPIRIT as a new creation in CHRIST JESUS, free of sin and sealed by the HOLY SPIRIT for the day of resurrection. When the believer dies, his or her soul goes straight to Heaven, and at the resurrection, the believer receives a new heavenly body like the one JESUS has. Unbelievers are also raised into an immortal body of some kind. They will face the White Throne Judgment and then an eternity in Hell (**Revelation 20:11-15**)

As a new creation in JESUS, the believer lives with GOD forever in paradise. Eternal life is the free gift of GOD, available to anyone who believes. GOD never takes back HIS gift. If you truly trust in JESUS alone to save your soul, you are sealed by the HOLY SPIRIT, who is ONE with GOD THE FATHER and THE SON, and your salvation can never be lost. You cannot be un-born again. JESUS is the giver of eternal life, and no one can snatch HIS sheep from HIS hand.

All other beliefs or attempts to reach Heaven trap a person in sin and mislead him or her to the Lake of Fire, known as Hell. GOD wishes none would perish eternally in Hell, which is why HE sent HIS own SON down from Heaven to buy our freedom with HIS perfect blood.

Claim GOD'S FREE GIFT to You Today!
Believe that JESUS is GOD IN FLESH. HE created you, and HE died on the cross to recreate you. HE was buried, and three days later rose into an immortal body. In JESUS alone, you're a new creation, free from sin and death, and fit for Heaven.

Ask GOD to forgive you and give you HIS free gift of eternal life in JESUS. Tell HIM you understand you're a sinner and have believed in JESUS' work on the cross to save you from sin, death, and an eternity in Hell. Try praying something like the prayer below. Please understand, this prayer doesn't save you. Only genuine trust in the death, burial, and resurrection of MESSIAH JESUS saves.

FATHER in Heaven,
   I have thought, spoken, and behaved in ways that are sinful. **I can't pay for my sins** by my own kindness or good deeds. I need you to take away my sins.
   I ask you to forgive me now. I receive your free gift of eternal life by receiving YOUR SON JESUS as my SAVIOR and LORD. **I believe YOU sent JESUS down from Heaven in the flesh and that JESUS willingly died on the cross for my sins. I believe**

21 DAYS OF EVANGELISM

JESUS was buried and rose to life on the third day. I believe JESUS is GOD IN FLESH, the MESSIAH, the SON OF GOD. JESUS is my **only** hope for the forgiveness of sins and everlasting life with YOU. JESUS, please baptize me with the **HOLY SPIRIT**, seal me for the day of resurrection, and fill me with the **HOLY SPIRIT**. Help me to give up all false beliefs and sin in my life. Help me to understand YOUR Word, the Holy Bible, and to live by it. **Thank you JESUS for saving me** from sin and eternal torment in Hell. Thank you for sealing me for the day of resurrection, when I will receive a body that will never die. Thank you for making me fit for Heaven as a new creation in CHRIST. Thank you GOD for making me **your child forever in JESUS CHRIST.**
In the name of JESUS, Amen.

What Happens if I Reject JESUS as the Only Way to Heaven?
Rejecting JESUS as the only way to Heaven will keep you trapped in sin and mislead you to eternal torment in the Lake of Fire, known as Hell. GOD wishes none would perish and sent HIS SON to save anyone who trusts in the blood of JESUS from having to go to Hell.

I Believe That Jesus Alone Is My Savior. Now What?
- **Keep believing** that JESUS is the **only** way to GOD THE FATHER.
- **Turn away from false beliefs,** false religions, man-made traditions, superstitions, practices the Bible forbids, fantasies, idols, and self-made beliefs.
- **Turn away from all sin**, such as anger, grudges, ingratitude, constant complaining, sexually immoral thoughts and deeds, profane and dirty speech, hateful thoughts and speech, gossip, substance abuse, selfishness, pride, greed, laziness, irresponsible spending, the consumption of empty media and entertainment, and over-indulgence in luxuries and nonessential pleasures of this life.
- **Stop trusting in your own efforts** and the people, products, and systems of this world for your security and happiness. Trust GOD alone to take care of you and fulfill your deepest longings.
- **Listen to the HOLY SPIRIT.** JESUS promises to send the HOLY SPIRIT to all who belong to Jesus. The HOLY SPIRIT

dwells with each believer, seals us for the day of resurrection, empowers us for ministry, and teaches us GOD's ways.
- **Live as a child of GOD**, talking to HIM continually in prayer. Listen to GOD by studying HIS word, the Bible, daily. If you've never read the Bible before, start with the Gospel of John. Worship GOD and pursue friendships with other believers. Try joining a local church and get baptized.
- Do as CHRIST commands in HIS great commission, and **tell everyone about JESUS**. Make disciples of JESUS.
- **Keep watching and praying** for the blessed appearance of CHRIST, at which time all who are in HIM will receive resurrected bodies, just as HE lives in a resurrected body.

How to Use This Book

The 21 tasks in this book are small enough that you can do one each day for 21 days. Each task should take roughly 15 minutes to complete, longer perhaps, if you haven't gathered your supplies ahead of time.

You may also break up the 21 tasks over a longer period of time, completing one assignment every few days or one per week. I recommend that you complete the tasks in the order given in this book, deviating only when necessary.

Please don't skip any assignments, and if you need to take a break, please pick up where you left off. It's too easy for us to say, "Oh, well, I missed that task. I guess I'll just skip it." Overcome your flesh by the resurrection power that's alive in you, and work diligently, as if you're working for JESUS HIMSELF—because you are.

This Book Is For Individuals and Groups.
Any Christian can use this book for his or her personal development in the area of evangelism. It can also be used by a church or group of Christians who want to grow in evangelism together. The 21 tasks can be completed as a group, in pairs, or individual group members can

complete the tasks independently and then report back to each other at regular group meetings.

For each assignment, I give group suggestions. These are intended to inspire Christian groups and their leaders to come up with their own ideas and ways of accomplishing the tasks.

Your group can go through all 21 tasks over a course of several weeks, or you can pick a few of the tasks and challenge your group to undertake them either individually or as a whole.

You may also split up or modify the assignments for any age or stage of people in your church or Christian group. For example, children can help their parents pack a blessing bag and accompany them with the delivery. **Please note:** Children should never be unattended when engaging in evangelism.

You can get your whole church, or a group within the church, involved in some of the evangelism tasks by asking the congregation to donate supplies or host a fundraiser to help covering the cost of Gospel tracts and Bibles. For example, the Youth Group could run a car wash or the women's ministry can run a bake sale.

Make These 21 Tasks a Natural Part of Your Day.
For long term success with evangelism, strive to make tasks like these 21 a natural part of your life. Every trip for groceries, each outing to the park, or meal at a restaurant, is a trip to a missions field. I promise, if you start thinking this way, you will see open doors for the Gospel everywhere.

Don't let the evangelism stop once you're through with this book. Use these 21 tasks a springboard into a lifetime of evangelism. Regularly repeat some of your favorite assignments, modifying them for different mission fields and situations. Get creative and come up with evangelism tasks of your own. As always, listen to the leading of the HOLY SPIRIT.

-1-
The Forgotten Basics of Evangelism

What Evangelism Is

Simply put, evangelism is the spoken or written proclamation of the Gospel of JESUS CHRIST.

Mark 16:15
And He said to them, "Go into all the world and preach the gospel to all creation."

In the fullest of terms, the Great Commission consists of four commands, which are mapped out in **Matthew 28:19-20**, a verse you can find in the next section of this book.
1. Go to everyone everywhere and make disciples of CHRIST.
2. Baptize disciples in the name of the FATHER, the SON, and the HOLY SPIRIT.
3. Teach everything JESUS commands.
4. Always remember that JESUS is with you, or in other words, do not fear.

This book focuses heavily on step 1 of the Great Commission, with the hopes of encouraging readers to do the most basic Christian work of "going" with the Gospel. The "going" is the part where most churches, and thereby Christians, fail. If we keep failing to initiate step 1 of the Great Commission, then we can never successfully accomplish any of the other steps. So let's start and at the beginning and get going.

What Is the Gospel?

If JESUS commands us to preach the Gospel, we must know exactly what the Gospel is. The Gospel is the good news that any human being can escape the fires of Hell and become a new creation, free of sin and death, by believing in the death, burial, and resurrection of JESUS CHRIST. As a new creation in JESUS, we will live with GOD forever in paradise. Eternal life, or salvation, is the free gift of GOD, available to anyone who trusts in the death, burial, and resurrection of JESUS as the only way to the FATHER in Heaven.

The Apostle Paul gives a perfect summary of the Gospel of JESUS CHRIST in **1 Corinthians 15:1-4**:

> [1] Now I make known to you, brethren, the gospel which I preached to you, which also you received, in which also you stand, [2] by which also you are saved, if you hold fast the word which I preached to you, unless you believed in vain. [3] For I delivered to you as of first importance what I also received, that Christ died for our sins according to the Scriptures, [4] and that He was buried, and that He was raised on the third day according to the Scriptures,

My Expanded Summary of the Gospel
Basically, we have all sinned and as a consequence, our bodies will die one day, and we will be condemned to eternal death in the Lake of Fire, known as Hell. GOD hates sin and death, and HE wishes none would perish. In HIS greatest act of mercy toward mankind, GOD sent HIS SON JESUS down from Heaven to cleanse our sin and give us new and immortal bodies.

JESUS paid for our sins when HE willingly shed HIS blood on the cross. JESUS is GOD IN FLESH, the perfect Passover LAMB OF GOD. Blood must atone for sin, and the blood of JESUS is the only acceptable payment for our sins. JESUS was buried and rose three days later into a body that will never die.

Anyone who believes this good news receives full forgiveness of sins and the promise of a new and immortal body at the resurrection. As recreated humans, sinless and immortal, we will live forever, as children of GOD, in paradise.

Eternal life in JESUS is the free gift of GOD. We can't earn eternal life by being kind or doing good deeds. We need to humble ourselves and receive by faith what JESUS did on the cross for us. We must accept the truth that only JESUS has the power to save us and bring us into HIS Kingdom because JESUS is the SON OF GOD, GOD IN FLESH, THE MESSIAH. Those who trust in the blood of JESUS alone have the future hope that we will live eternally with GOD.

What Evangelism Isn't

In these end times, Christians everywhere have turned away from GOD's pure and simple model of evangelism as given in the Bible, and we have accumulated all kinds of false teachings about what we think evangelism is. In fact, for the past several decades, perhaps longer, churches have been teaching a false evangelism. False evangelism looks a lot like actual evangelism except it completely flips upside-down GOD's prescribed order of operations. False evangelism instruction says to build relationships, dine, and invest in people before telling them about JESUS. True evangelism instruction says to go and proclaim JESUS. Build relationships with those who receive HIM.

Despite its diametric opposition to the Bible, false evangelism has been prevailing over true Biblical instruction because it appeals to our flesh, which is at war with the SPIRIT. The HOLY SPIRIT prompts us to follow JESUS' Great Commission—to go into the world in faith and proclaim the Gospel to every creature. The flesh hates the very thought of doing such a thing. It seems rude and crude, and even insulting to our intelligence to just go out into public and proclaim the Gospel. Our flesh would rather stay inside the four walls of a church building and complete tasks that look kind of like evangelism, but are really just creative ways of pandering to and socializing with the world.

The flesh, therefore, loves false teachings about evangelism. The flesh naturally gravitates towards activities that delay, complicate, and puff up the Great Commission. The flesh likes the idea of taking an unbeliever out to lunch, doing an act of service, running a quasi-Gospel course, and hosting community events in lieu of hitting the streets with the message of the cross. The flesh thinks it's a great idea to show an unbeliever we care by sitting down with her and listening attentively as she spouts off fantastical lies about what she thinks happens after death.

False "evangelistic" activities like the ones described here fool the Christian into investing time and money into "potential prospects." False evangelism encourages us to make our "prospects" feel warm and fuzzy before bringing up the topic of JESUS. False evangelism encourages us to share our personal testimony before we get around to sharing the only testimony that has the power to save a soul from an eternity in Hell— CHRIST's testimony. (I will touch on how to use personal testimony in a healthy way later.) These heretical approaches to evangelism steal time, money, and resources that we could otherwise invest in true Biblical evangelism.

False evangelism also causes Christians to yoke ourselves to unbelievers, to entangle ourselves in religious pyramid schemes, to fellowship with darkness, to pollute ourselves by pursuing unholy matrimony with the world, and to ultimately miss out on eternal rewards. Satan loves it when Christians pollute themselves and voluntarily steal their own resources by needlessly offering free meals and therapy sessions because we are self-deceived into thinking that such activities qualify as evangelism. When we boil down false evangelism its the core, we find Satan at dead center.

Below are just a few counterfeit "evangelistic" activities you will want to avoid. These activities look like evangelism, just as Satan appears as an angel of light. But these models for evangelism, like Satan, will steal, kill, and destroy if you allow them to dominate your ministry style. If only we would stick to GOD's straight and narrow path…

Relationship Building Is Not Evangelism.
The *relationship-first* model for any ministry, especially evangelism, is perhaps the deadliest of all to the Christian faith. Relationships are a blessing from GOD, but building relationships with unbelievers, with the intention of sharing JESUS later, oftentimes traps Christians into unhealthy relationships with unbelievers and causes us to delay our Gospel sharing too long. In many cases, the *relationship-first* model for ministry misleads us into not sharing JESUS at all.

You might as well be as authentic as possible when you first meet someone, and share JESUS upfront. That's the only thing that really matters, isn't it? If the person rejects JESUS, you are not obligated to invest anything in that person other than prayer and a helping hand when needed (**Matthew 5:43-45, Romans 12:20**). And now that person will know exactly to whom she can turn if and when she starts thinking about eternity.

Please, pray for those who reject JESUS, and do minister to them in times of crises. However, you need not invite a GOD-rejecter into your home, treat her to lunch, or engage in relationship building with her. You would never knowingly invite an unrepentant murderer into your home. In GOD's eyes, rejecting the blood of HIS SON is a worse sin than murder. In fact, the rejection of JESUS is the greatest sin a human can commit. It's the only sin that's unforgiveable. Stop inviting unrepentant rejecters of JESUS into your life. If you have a chance to minister to such people as you engage with them during the natural course of your day, then by all means, take those opportunities, but please don't create opportunities to fellowship with darkness.

Build Relationships With Gospel-Receivers. Minister at a Distance to Gospel-Rejecters.
The Bible explicitly tells Christians not to linger where the Gospel is rejected, but rather, to build our relationships with those who receive JESUS (**Matthew 10:11-14**). Our closest relationships should be built with other believers for the purposes of discipling and building each other up. People who do the will of GOD are our actual family members, and we should treat them as such (**Matthew 12:50**). Our Brothers and Sisters in CHRIST are the people with whom we should be dining and inviting into our intimate spaces. JESUS HIMSELF modeled this for us (**John 1:38-41**). HE ministered to many people, but HE most frequently and most intimately ate and lodged with HIS twelve, teaching them all they would need for ministry when HE was no longer with them in body.

Do as JESUS did, and teach the Gospel first. Then, dine with those who thirst for more of JESUS. When we reverse the order of these activities, dining with unbelievers before sharing the Gospel, what we're doing is forming bonds with people who have not asked for more of JESUS. We have no idea if this person has never heard about JESUS or if she's heard the Gospel 20 times and has willfully rejected the blood of the SON OF GOD. If we take just 30 seconds to talk to new people in our lives about JESUS, we would know immediately whether to minister to them up close or at a distance.

For example, if you're not sure if a person has or hasn't heard the Gospel before, then present JESUS to the that person in a neutral setting, such as a parking lot or breakroom. Inviting a person to coffee is low-cost, but still, I recommend against any kind of table fellowship or one-on-one bonding with anyone unless you know the person is interested in learning more about JESUS. If an unbeliever invites you to fellowship, and you want to go, please use discretion (**1 Corinthians 10:27**). **Be informed:** Your employer may have rules that prohibit talking about religion during work hours, but no one can govern what you say in private conversation on your own time. Also, there may come a time when you must choose between following GOD or losing your job. Always ask GOD for HIS wisdom. He promises to give wisdom without reproach (**James 1:5**).

As mentioned earlier, the Bible instructs us against forming bonds with unbelievers (**1 Corinthians 15:33**), and JESUS models for us that we are to proclaim the Gospel to the lost and disciple those who want to be found. The people who realize they need a doctor are the ones who will stay to receive the physician's blessings. Those are the people with whom we should dine. We don't need to invite into our homes people who have already rejected the doctor's orders—unless, of course, those people repent and come around seeking the cure.

JESUS Didn't Dine With Sinners the Way We Think.
You might argue that JESUS built a relationship with Judas, who was an unbeliever. You are correct. Out of obedience to the FATHER, JESUS stayed in close fellowship with Judas because someone from HIS inner circle would have to betray HIM. JESUS had to get to the cross somehow, and HE kept fellowship with Judas unto that end. JESUS loved Judas, even though HE knew Judas was a devil from the beginning, and treated him well up until the bitter end. The close relationship between Judas and JESUS, however, does not give Christians the license to knowingly keep close fellowship with unbelievers. We do as the Bible instructs: We evangelize unbelievers and build relationships with Gospel-receivers.

You might also argue that JESUS dined with tax collectors and sinners. Remember, this was an accusation made against JESUS by the Pharisees who were looking for any which way to criticize and malign HIM (**Matthew 9, Mark 2, Luke 5**). More accurately, JESUS dined with repentant sinners who realized they needed forgiveness. HE did not go carousing in bars and brothels, building relationships with each and every sinner in an attempt to someday share the Good News of the Kingdom. HE went from town to town proclaiming the words of eternal life preforming miracles for all who came to HIM.

Moreover, the sinners who hosted JESUS in their homes, namely Matthew and Zacchaeus, had already turned away from their former ways and committed to following HIM. True, the other guests at these dinner parties may have still been in sin, but to remedy that JESUS spent most of HIS time teaching and ministering to such folks, not building close relationships with them.

The only instances recorded when JESUS intentionally dined with unrepentant sinners were when HE went into the homes of Pharisees (**Luke 7 and 14**). For instance, at the dinner party hosted by Simon the Pharisee in **Luke 7**, JESUS confronted the sin and hypocrisy of HIS Pharisaic host, and HE created quite a scene when HE received a blessing from a wayward woman and forgave her sins. JESUS never buttered up a person over a meal before confronting sin and calling the person to repentance. HE confronted sin head on, and HE reserved forgiveness and miracles for those who realized they needed a physician.

False Evangelism is Like a Pyramid Scheme.
How does it make you feel when you're invited to a friend's house for what you think is a party and then someone whips out a display of gimmicky products and asks you to buy? This is kind of what it's like when you invite someone to your house or for a meal and then spring the Gospel on them.

If you evangelize according to GOD's model, you will never have to worry about having to strategically deceive someone in this way. When people see you on the sidewalk with your Gospel sign and JESUS t-shirt, they will know exactly what they're getting into. If a person on the street is repulsed by your Gospel sign, then he or she is not being drawn to JESUS just yet. That person will walk on by, and you will have not wasted any time or money inviting her to a meal and forming a bond with her with the hopes of one day whipping out your Gospel presentation. Think of all the time and resources you'll save by not investing in not-ready people. You can then take those resources and invest them into people who actually come to the fountain for living water.

Note: If an unbeliever in your life has approached you and wants to know about JESUS, that person is obviously being drawn by to GOD. Go ahead and share the cross of JESUS with her (over coffee or a meal if you prefer). If the person accepts JESUS, you can disciple her and build a relationship. If she rejects the Gospel, you are not obligated to invest anything more than prayer, cordial conversations in passing, follow up information about JESUS when opportunities arise, and emergency assistance when needed.

Prioritizing Goods and Services Over the Gospel is Manipulation, Not Evangelism (Unless You're Helping the Poor).
Many well-respected church leaders and evangelists will tell you to offer something tangible to people before presenting the Gospel. These teachers will suggest you take people to a meal, invite them into your home, clean their toilet, or mow their lawn before even mentioning the name of JESUS—the only name given to mankind that can save. It's not a bad idea to serve others, but only if you share JESUS first. JESUS is our head. HE must have first place in all we do (**Colossians 1:15-18**).

Also, JESUS has given us all authority to proclaim the Gospel. Please read the Great Commission Bible verses listed out later in this chapter. If we have all authority from GOD to proclaim the Gospel, we don't need to bribe people with goods and services to make sure we can go and do GOD's work.

Personal Note: When evangelizing I offer free prayer as a means of casting my net. If people respond to the offer, I lead the conversation with an explanation of why I pray in the name of JESUS, and I give a Gospel presentation. If the person sticks around (and ideally professes faith), then I send her off with Christian literature, a Bible if needed, and sometimes a goodie bag or small gift. Even though I offer goods, first place is given to the Gospel. In scenarios like this, the goods or services are an added blessing for those who abide and listen to the Gospel message. They're not the main feature. The only time I freely hand out goodie bags without engaging in a Gospel conversation is if I'm evangelizing in a location where people are quickly passing by, and the goodie bags always contain a Gospel tract.

The Exception to This Rule.
When ministering to hungry and needy people, and the fatherless, we should be offering free meals, goods, and services because we are helping to meet basic needs. The Bible commands us to help the poor in this way. See the appropriate verses listed out later in this chapter.

I almost always offer goods and services to gain entry into poor communities, but I make it clear when offering services to the poor that I do so in the name of JESUS. And I always proclaim the Gospel to these communities. **Personal Note:** The poor are generally receptive to the Gospel. Praise GOD!

Conversely, hosting something like a Harvest Festival at your church with the hopes of winning families back to your property on a Sunday morning is not meeting a basic need for anybody. If you have evangelistic activities at the festival and someone delivers a clear Gospel presentation to the crowd, then great. That's evangelistic. If not, your festival is essentially a waste of church resources. Even if you attract a family or two to your church, you've wasted an opportunity to share JESUS with the dozens of families who will probably never return to your property unless there's cotton candy and a bouncy house.

Being a Good Example Is Not Evangelism.
Many church leaders wrongly teach that our life example is our evangelism to the world. These teachers will falsely instruct congregants to "only use words if necessary" when proclaiming the Gospel. Imagine if JESUS followed this method. We would be missing from our Bibles the very words of eternal life!

Of course Christians should seek to live exemplary lives. That's called *pursuing holiness*, but it's not evangelism. Evangelism requires the Gospel to be spoken or published for others to hear or read. It's fine to use pictures and visual dramatizations to aid with your Gospel presentation, but this fact remains: The transformative power of the death, burial, and resurrection of JESUS must be communicated with words.

I challenge you to search the Bible and try to find any message GOD has ever given to any of HIS servants that HE did not intend to be publicized or read out loud for others to hear. The only exceptions I can think of are two accounts of the sealing up of end times prophecies in the books of Daniel and Revelation (**Daniel 12:4, Revelation 10:1-4**).

The very existence of the Bible in print is evidence that GOD wants HIS word to be read and heard. You might argue that the point of hearing GOD's word is to become doers of the word, and doing GOD's word means being a good example to others. This is partially true. The other part of that truth is that "doing" GOD's word means making disciples of JESUS through Gospel declaration.

Winning People to Yourself Is Not Evangelism.
I can't believe I have to address this issue, but I do. Some churches wrongly teach that Christians must win people to themselves through a sparkling personality and good deeds before they can win them to JESUS. Our personality, witty talk, and good deeds are not the power of GOD to save. In fact, we have nothing to do with winning souls, other than dying to ourselves so we can be vessels for the one and only thing that does win souls—the Gospel of JESUS (**Luke 9:23**).

Teaching people that they need to win others to themselves before sharing the Gospel is arrogant, heretical, and downright devilish. Of course Christians should be courteous and respectful to all humans, but the Bible is clear that no matter how kind we are, we will be despised by the world (**2 Timothy 3:12**). Most people are offended and repulsed by actual Christians. The only kind of "Christians" the world likes are the fake kind, who flatter others, give bribes, teach a false Gospel, avoid or grossly delay bringing up JESUS, and those who never talk about sin, judgement, death, or Hell. Christians, as I once learned from a random *YouTube* post, we are to be the salt of the earth, not sugar.

False Evangelism Listens. True Evangelism Proclaims.
Many church leaders falsely teach that Christians must listen to people before proclaiming the Gospel to them. While it can help to ask a few questions when engaging in a Gospel conversation, such as "What is your spiritual upbringing?" and "How does a person get to Heaven?," JESUS commands us to go and proclaim the Gospel, not to go and listen to people talk about everything except the Gospel with the hopes of someday getting our turn to speak. JESUS already gave us all authority to speak when HE gave the Great Commission.

As you engage in more and more Gospel conversations, you will be able to identify a person's false beliefs in a matter of seconds of listening to her speak. The HOLY SPIRIT will then direct your Gospel presentation to that particular person. You need not let a person ramble on and on about nonsense, such as Viking gods, avatars, evolution, a sin-tolerant "Jesus," and fantastical stories about what happens to people when they die. Out of love and respect for that person, you will end his or her nonsense speech and immediately administer the only truth that can heal a depraved mind—the Gospel of JESUS.

You would never let a good friend of yours embarrass herself by talking gibberish to others. If you love your friend, you would be concerned if she was speaking nonsense. Her fantastical speech would tell you something was wrong with her mind and that she needed help. In the same way, if you truly love a person who holds nonsense beliefs, and you know the only cure is JESUS, indulging the person's nonsense, when you could otherwise be sharing the Gospel, is not loving at all. In fact, it's cruel.

Follow JESUS' model. HE spoke to people way more than HE listened to them during HIS ministry on earth. JESUS was considered a rabbi, and people flocked to hear HIM teach, not to get therapy sessions from HIM. During HIS earthly ministry, JESUS lectured constantly because HE knew HIS words held the power of eternal life (**John 5:24**). JESUS never indulged lies or endured unholy conversations with the hopes of getting HIS chance to speak. HE actualized HIS divine authority and spoke. If the people you encounter don't like being lectured about the Gospel, they probably won't like JESUS. The only way to find out is to proclaim the Good News and see how they react.

Personal Note: I suspect the only time JESUS did more listening than speaking was when He was in the presence of THE FATHER in prayer.

You might argue that the Bible tells us to be quick to listen and slow to speak (**James 1:19-20, Proverbs 18:13**). This is true when we are engaged in personal conversations or potential arguments. If we are sharing the Gospel, however, the command is to go in the authority of JESUS CHRIST and proclaim, preach, speak, teach, and undertake any other verbal action necessary to make disciples of JESUS. We need not be slow to speak when sharing the Gospel with those who are abysmally lost and have never heard the only message that can save their souls.

Your Personal Testimony May Hinder JESUS' Testimony.
Personal testimony is great to use when evangelizing, but you don't have to use it all the time (or at all). It's JESUS' testimony that saves souls. A simple explanation of the death, burial, and resurrection of JESUS is all anyone needs to understand the free gift of eternal life available to her in CHRIST.

Personal Note: If and when I use my personal testimony, I usually sprinkle in tiny snippets as the SPIRIT leads. I have found that when I use too much personal testimony, I risk running out of time to share JESUS' testimony. I use personal testimony most often when suggesting someone seeks deliverance from harassing spirits. JESUS freed me personally from many demons, and I wish that everyone would find the freedom and healing JESUS can give them through deliverance. People are generally more willing to learn about deliverance when they hear personal testimonies. If you're interested in learning more about deliverance and miracles, you can start by looking up videos of Derek Prince, Frank Hammond, Vlad Savchuck, and Tom Loud.

Church Promotion Is Not Evangelism.
Plenty of people will post signs on their front lawn advertising their church or Christian school of choice, but many of these people will recoil at the idea of putting up a Gospel sign. Churches will hire marketers and administrators who will to push their church brand, design t-shirts, and toil to make a church logo, but you would be hard-pressed to find an evangelist on staff at any given church in the United States. At best, you

will find an outreach coordinator, who spends the bulk of her time trying to get people to attend events, organizing services for the community, giving out goods, but never giving out the one thing JESUS told us to give out—the Gospel.

Brothers and sisters, please **be informed**, church promotion and church programs are not evangelism. The only things we can take to Heaven with us are human souls, and the only thing that has the power to get souls into Heaven is the Gospel. Everything else will burn like chaff before the judgment throne.

Hosting a Course Can Prevent or Delay Gospel Proclamation.
There's nothing wrong with running courses about JESUS, and such courses can be great for discipling new believes. But please make sure not to confuse JESUS courses with evangelism. A course is a course. Evangelism is evangelism. Yes, people get saved taking courses because the word of GOD cuts to the soul and never returns void. If you want your course to have an evangelistic element to it, which every course should, then please open the course with the Gospel, and reinforce the Gospel at every session.

Just think about how much joy it gives Satan when a church runs a six-week course about JESUS, but doesn't encourage the attendees to commit to JESUS until week six. Think of all the people who could drop out by week four or miss the Gospel presentation at the end. Opening or closing class sessions with the Gospel is simpler to do than many people realize. A full Gospel explanation can take as little as two minutes to present, and if a person is ready to receive JESUS, it takes less than two seconds for her to get saved. If you run a JESUS course with the intention of seeing people get saved, please don't wait until week six to give your altar call, and have baptisms scheduled continually.

Inviting People to Church Is (Usually) Good, But It's Not Evangelism.
People get saved hearing the Gospel at church, so if your church faithfully preaches the Gospel, then by all means, invite anyone who will come. The sad reality is that many churches today do not present the Gospel at every service, or at all. When you invite people to church, you're inviting them to your particular brand of Christianity, and that

brand may or may not be in line with the Bible. It's always best to invite people to JESUS first. Share the Gospel, not your brand.

Supporting Evangelism is Good, But It's Not Evangelism.
Sending and supporting missionaries and evangelists is great, but it does not absolve you of evangelizing. Financially supporting others is an exercise in giving, not Gospel proclamation. Even if you give generously to missions, you are still accountable for sharing JESUS with your friends, family, colleagues, new believers, children and youth in your church, your community, and every other creature you encounter. (See The Great Commission verses listed later in this chapter.)

If a Christian Anywhere in the World Can't Replicate It, Then It's Probably Not Evangelism.
One of the reasons why GOD's Great Commission is so pure and simple is that it can be successfully completed by any Christian (even those who are new to the faith), anywhere in the world, at any time. The same evangelism model that worked for Peter and Paul is guaranteed to work for us. There will always be persecution and obstacles to evangelism, but obstacles aside, if the model you're using to reach people with the Gospel can't be used by a Brother or Sister who doesn't have a Bible or a pair of shoes, then the model is most likely not of GOD.

Even in the poorest of countries, our brothers and sisters can take the Gospel from village to village by plain and simple word-of-mouth. We pray all of our brethren will get Bibles, but many Christians possess only the spoken testimony of the death, burial, and resurrection of JESUS, and that's all they need to start evangelizing. That's all any Christian needs.

If GOD blesses us with resources and technologies, and we are able to find creative ways to share the Gospel, then praise GOD! It is still our top priority to do the one thing that can be done by any Christian anywhere—proclaim the Gospel of JESUS CHRIST. For example, if you have the resources and are able to hand-deliver stress relief kits to college students during exams and share the Gospel with them, then do it. Keep in mind, however, you don't need to offer such kits. The kits are an added bonus to your evangelism, but by no means a necessity. And never let the lack of such resources deter you from doing what Christians all around the globe do—preach the Gospel.

Keep the main thing the main thing, and the main thing is always the Gospel of JESUS. The Gospel is the power of GOD to save, and that's the best thing you can offer to anyone. In the words of Peter who understood that GOD's power is infinitely greater than any riches on earth,

> **Acts 3:6**
> "I do not possess silver and gold, but what I do have I give to you: In the name of Jesus Christ the Nazarene—walk!"

If GOD blesses us with resources, we are expected to use all HE gives us to serve the Gospel of JESUS, and we must not fool ourselves into thinking that Gospel-less church activities are evangelism. An impoverished brother or sister would never dream of being frivolous. If an impoverished brother or sister would disapprove of our ministry activity, then it's probably not of GOD, and it's almost certainly not evangelism.

Let GOD HIMSELF Teach You About Evangelism.

Christians, we are sanctified by the word of GOD because the word of GOD is truth (**John 17:17**). Let the word of GOD work in you. Let GOD teach you directly, mouth to mouth, breath to breath, SPIRIT to spirit. Mediate on the following verses about evangelism. Try memorizing a few of them. Maybe make it a goal to memorize one verse each week.

Before you study these verses, ask GOD to teach you how HE defines evangelism. GOD loves when we consult HIM first and foremost in all matters of life, especially in wanting to learn more about HIS book and HIS work of Gospel proclamation.

Our Great Commission from JESUS

> **Matthew 28:19-20**
> [19]"Go therefore and make disciples of all the nations, baptizing them in the name of the Father and the Son and the Holy Spirit, [20]teaching them to observe all that I commanded you; and lo, I am with you always, even to the end of the age."

Mark 16:15-18

[15] And He said to them, "Go into all the world and preach the gospel to all creation. [16] He who has believed and has been baptized shall be saved; but he who has disbelieved shall be condemned. [17] These signs will accompany those who have believed: in My name they will cast out demons, they will speak with new tongues; [18] they will pick up serpents, and if they drink any deadly *poison*, it will not hurt them; they will lay hands on the sick, and they will recover."

Luke 24:46-48

[46] and He said to them, "Thus it is written, that the Christ would suffer and rise again from the dead the third day, [47] and that repentance for forgiveness of sins would be proclaimed in His name to all the nations, beginning from Jerusalem. [48] You are witnesses of these things.

Acts 1:8

but you will receive power when the Holy Spirit has come upon you; and you shall be My witnesses both in Jerusalem, and in all Judea and Samaria, and even to the remotest part of the earth."

2 Timothy 2:2

The things which you have heard from me in the presence of many witnesses, entrust these to faithful men who will be able to teach others also

2 Timothy 4:1-5

[1] I solemnly charge *you* in the presence of God and of Christ Jesus, who is to judge the living and the dead, and by His appearing and His kingdom: [2] preach the word; be ready in season *and* out of season; reprove, rebuke, exhort, with great patience and instruction. [3] For the time will come when they will not endure sound doctrine; but *wanting* to have their ears tickled, they will accumulate for themselves teachers in accordance to their own desires, [4] and will turn away their ears from the truth and will turn aside to myths. [5] But you, be

sober in all things, endure hardship, do the work of an evangelist, fulfill your ministry.

Evangelism Is How Christians Continue JESUS' Earthly Ministry
We Are HIS Body on Earth. What Would JESUS Do? Evangelize!

Isaiah 61:1-2 (We continue JESUS' mission as HIS body.)
[1] The Spirit of the Lord GOD is upon me,
Because the LORD has anointed me
To bring good news to the afflicted;
He has sent me to bind up the brokenhearted,
To proclaim liberty to captives
And freedom to prisoners;
[2] To proclaim the favorable year of the LORD
And the day of vengeance of our God;
To comfort all who mourn,

2 Corinthians 5:20
Therefore, we are ambassadors for Christ, as though God were making an appeal through us; we beg you on behalf of Christ, be reconciled to God.

The Gospel Itself Is the Power of GOD to Save.

Isaiah 55:11
So will My word be which goes forth from My mouth;
It will not return to Me empty,
Without accomplishing what I desire,
And without succeeding *in the matter* for which I sent it.

Romans 1:16
For I am not ashamed of the gospel, for it is the power of God for salvation to everyone who believes, to the Jew first and also to the Greek.

1 Corinthians 1:18
For the word of the cross is foolishness to those who are perishing, but to us who are being saved it is the power of God.

Hebrews 4:12
For the word of God is living and active and sharper than any two-edged sword, and piercing as far as the division of soul and spirit, of both joints and marrow, and able to judge the thoughts and intentions of the heart.

GOD Guarantees HE Will Save People When the Gospel Is Proclaimed (Even When It Seems Everyone Rejects It).

Matthew 9:37
Then He said to His disciples, "The harvest is plentiful, but the workers are few. [38] Therefore beseech the Lord of the harvest to send out workers into His harvest."

John 4:35-36
[35] Do you not say, 'There are yet four months, and *then* comes the harvest'? Behold, I say to you, lift up your eyes and look on the fields, that they are white for harvest. [36] Already he who reaps is receiving wages and is gathering fruit for life eternal; so that he who sows and he who reaps may rejoice together.

Acts 18:9-10
[9] And the Lord said to Paul in the night by a vision, "Do not be afraid *any longer*, but go on speaking and do not be silent; [10] for I am with you, and no man will attack you in order to harm you, for I have many people in this city."

2 Corinthians 2:15-16
[15] For we are a fragrance of Christ to God among those who are being saved and among those who are perishing; [16] to the one an aroma from death to death, to the other an aroma from life to life.

Galatians 6:9
Let us not lose heart in doing good, for in due time we will reap if we do not grow weary.

We Are to Boldly and Publicly Proclaim JESUS.

Proverbs 1:20-21
[20] Wisdom shouts in the street,
She lifts her voice in the square;
[21] At the head of the noisy *streets* she cries out;
At the entrance of the gates in the city she utters her sayings:

Matthew 10:27
What I tell you in the darkness, speak in the light; and what you hear *whispered* in *your* ear, proclaim upon the housetops.

Acts 4:29
And now, Lord, take note of their threats, and grant that Your bond-servants may speak Your word with all confidence,

See **Romans 1:16**, listed earlier.

2 Timothy 1:8
Therefore do not be ashamed of the testimony of our Lord or of me His prisoner, but join with *me* in suffering for the gospel according to the power of God,

The Gospel Must Be Spoken (or Written) With Words.

Romans 10:13-15
[13] for "WHOEVER WILL CALL ON THE NAME OF THE LORD WILL BE SAVED." [14] How then will they call on Him in whom they have not believed? How will they believe in Him whom they have not heard? And how will they hear without a preacher? [15] How will they preach unless they are sent?

Miracles, Signs, and Wonders Accompany True Evangelism.

See **Mark 16:15-18**, listed earlier.

Luke 9:1-2
[1] And He called the twelve together, and gave them power and authority over all the demons and to heal diseases. [2] And

He sent them out to proclaim the kingdom of God and to perform healing.

Acts 4:29-30
...grant that Your bond-servants may speak Your word with all confidence, [30] while You [GOD] extend Your hand to heal, and signs and wonders take place through the name of Your holy servant Jesus.

1 Corinthians 2:4-5
[4] and my message and my preaching were not in persuasive words of wisdom, but in demonstration of the Spirit and of power, [5] so that your faith would not rest on the wisdom of men, but on the power of God.

1 Corinthians 4:20
[18] Now some have become arrogant, as though I were not coming to you. [19] But I will come to you soon, if the Lord wills, and I shall find out, not the words of those who are arrogant but their power. [20] For the kingdom of God does not consist in words but in power.

2 Corinthians 12:12
The distinguishing marks of a true apostle were performed among you with all perseverance, by signs, wonders, and miracles.

1 Thessalonians 1:5
for our gospel did not come to you in word only, but also in power and in the Holy Spirit and with full conviction; just as you know what kind of men we proved to be among you for your sake.

Hebrews 2:3-4
[3] how will we escape if we neglect so great a salvation? After it was at the first spoken through the Lord, it was confirmed to us by those who heard, [4] God also testifying with them, both by signs and wonders and by various miracles and by gifts of the Holy Spirit according to His own will.

Fear Is Not From GOD and Must Be Driven Away.

2 Timothy 1:7
For God has not given us a spirit of timidity, but of power and love and discipline.

1 John 4:18
There is no fear in love; but perfect love casts out fear, because fear involves punishment, and the one who fears is not perfected in love.

We Must Pray for Evangelism.

Matthew 9:38
Therefore beseech the Lord of the harvest to send out workers into His harvest."

Ephesians 6:19-20
[19] and *pray* on my behalf, that utterance may be given to me in the opening of my mouth, to make known with boldness the mystery of the gospel, [20] for which I am an ambassador in chains; that in *proclaiming* it I may speak boldly, as I ought to speak.

Colossians 4:2-5
[2] Devote yourselves to prayer, keeping alert in it with *an attitude of* thanksgiving; [3] praying at the same time for us as well, that God will open up to us a door for the word, so that we may speak forth the mystery of Christ, for which I have also been imprisoned; [4] that I may make it clear in the way I ought to speak.

2 Thessalonians 3:1-2
[1] Finally, brethren, pray for us that the word of the Lord will spread rapidly and be glorified, just as *it did* also with you; [2] and that we will be rescued from perverse and evil men; for not all have faith.

Not Evangelizing is a Sin and Has Eternal Consequences.

Ezekiel 3:18-19
[18] When I say to the wicked, 'You will surely die,' and you do not warn him or speak out to warn the wicked from his wicked way that he may live, that wicked man shall die in his iniquity, but his blood I will require at your hand. [19] Yet if you have warned the wicked and he does not turn from his wickedness or from his wicked way, he shall die in his iniquity; but you have delivered yourself.

Matthew 10:32-33
[32] "Therefore everyone who confesses Me before men, I will also confess him before My Father who is in heaven. [33] But whoever denies Me before men, I will also deny him before My Father who is in heaven.

There is a Crown to be Earned For Evangelizing.

1 Thessalonians 2:19
For who is our hope or joy or crown of exultation? Is it not even you, in the presence of our Lord Jesus at His coming?

Philippians 4:1
Therefore, my beloved brethren whom I long *to see*, my joy and crown, in this way stand firm in the Lord, my beloved.

Follow JESUS for Your Training.

Matthew 4:19-20
[19] And He said to them, "Follow Me, and I will make you fishers of men." [20] Immediately they left their nets and followed Him.

Acts 4:13
Now as they observed the confidence of Peter and John and understood that they were uneducated and untrained men, they were amazed, and *began* to recognize them as having been with Jesus.

Don't Build Relationships Where the Gospel Is Rejected.

Psalm 101:4-5
[4] A froward heart shall depart from me: I will not know a wicked person.
[5] Whoso privily slandereth his neighbour, him will I cut off: him that hath an high look and a proud heart will not I suffer. (KJV)

Psalm 119:63
I am a companion of all those who fear You,
And of those who keep Your precepts.

Matthew 10:14
Whoever does not receive you, nor heed your words, as you go out of that house or that city, shake the dust off your feet.

1 Corinthians 15:33
Do not be deceived: "Bad company corrupts good morals."

2 Corinthians 6:14-15
[14] Do not be bound together with unbelievers; for what partnership have righteousness and lawlessness, or what fellowship has light with darkness? [15] Or what harmony has Christ with Belial, or what has a believer in common with an unbeliever?

We Must Make Sacrifices for Kingdom Work.

Matthew 19:29
And everyone who has left houses or brothers or sisters or father or mother or children or farms for My name's sake, will receive many times as much, and will inherit eternal life.

Luke 9:23-24
[23] And He was saying to *them* all, "If anyone wishes to come after Me, he must deny himself, and take up his cross daily and follow Me. [24] For whoever wishes to save his life will lose it,

but whoever loses his life for My sake, he is the one who will save it.

JESUS Promises Evangelism Is Not a Heavy Burden. HE Is Always With Us.

Isaiah 41:10 & 13
[10] 'Do not fear, for I am with you;
Do not anxiously look about you, for I am your God.
I will strengthen you, surely I will help you,
Surely I will uphold you with My righteous right hand.[…]
[13] "For I am the LORD your God, who upholds your right hand,
Who says to you, 'Do not fear, I will help you.'

Matthew 11:28-30
[28] "Come to Me, all who are weary and heavy-laden, and I will give you rest. [29] Take My yoke upon you and learn from Me, for I am gentle and humble in heart, and YOU WILL FIND REST FOR YOUR SOULS. [30] For My yoke is easy and My burden is light."

(See Great Commission verse Matthew 28:20.)

You Will Suffer Persecution for Gospel Work.

Matthew 5:11-12
[11] "Blessed are you when *people* insult you and persecute you, and falsely say all kinds of evil against you because of Me. [12] Rejoice and be glad, for your reward in heaven is great; for in this same way they persecuted the prophets who were before you.

Matthew 10:16
Behold, I send you out as sheep in the midst of wolves; so be shrewd as serpents and innocent as doves.

Matthew 10:22
You will be hated by all because of My name, but it is the one who has endured to the end who will be saved.

John 15:18
"If the world hates you, you know that it has hated Me before *it hated* you.

See **2 Corinthians 2:15-16**, listed earlier.

Philippians 1:29
For to you it has been granted for Christ's sake, not only to believe in Him, but also to suffer for His sake,

2 Timothy 3:12
Indeed, all who desire to live godly in Christ Jesus will be persecuted.

1 Corinthians 4:11-14
[11] To this present hour we are both hungry and thirsty, and are poorly clothed, and are roughly treated, and are homeless; [12] and we toil, working with our own hands; when we are reviled, we bless; when we are persecuted, we endure; [13] when we are slandered, we try to conciliate; we have become as the scum of the world, the dregs of all things, *even* until now.

1 Peter 4:12-14
[12] Beloved, do not be surprised at the fiery ordeal among you, which comes upon you for your testing, as though some strange thing were happening to you; [13] but to the degree that you share the sufferings of Christ, keep on rejoicing, so that also at the revelation of His glory you may rejoice with exultation. [14] If you are reviled for the name of Christ, you are blessed, because the Spirit of glory and of God rests on you.

Satan Blinds People to the Gospel. Pray for Those Who Reject JESUS, That They Will See and Be Saved.

John 12:39-40
[39] For this reason they could not believe, for Isaiah said again, [40] "HE HAS BLINDED THEIR EYES AND HE HARDENED THEIR HEART, SO THAT THEY WOULD NOT SEE WITH THEIR

EYES AND PERCEIVE WITH THEIR HEART, AND BE CONVERTED AND I HEAL THEM."

2 Corinthians 4:3-4
[3] And even if our gospel is veiled, it is veiled to those who are perishing, [4] in whose case the god of this world has blinded the minds of the unbelieving so that they might not see the light of the gospel of the glory of Christ, who is the image of God.

We Must Pray for Our Persecutors and Meet Their Basic Needs if Given the Opportunity.

Matthew 5:44-45
[44] But I say to you, love your enemies and pray for those who persecute you, [45] so that you may be sons of your Father who is in heaven;

Romans 12:19-21 (Quoted from Proverbs 25:21-22)
[19] Never take your own revenge, beloved, but leave room for the wrath *of God*, for it is written, "VENGEANCE IS MINE, I WILL REPAY," says the Lord. [20] "BUT IF YOUR ENEMY IS HUNGRY, FEED HIM, AND IF HE IS THIRSTY, GIVE HIM A DRINK; FOR IN SO DOING YOU WILL HEAP BURNING COALS ON HIS HEAD." [21] Do not be overcome by evil, but overcome evil with good.

True Evangelism Will Divide Families.

Mark 6:4
Jesus said to them, "A prophet is not without honor except in his hometown and among his relatives and in his own household."

Luke 4:24
And He said, "Truly I say to you, no prophet is welcome in his hometown.

Luke 12:51-53

[51] Do you suppose that I came to grant peace on earth? I tell you, no, but rather division; [52] for from now on five *members* in one household will be divided, three against two and two against three. [53] They will be divided, father against son and son against father, mother against daughter and daughter against mother, mother-in-law against daughter-in-law and daughter-in-law against mother-in-law."

Biblical Evangelism Looks Weak and Foolish to the World.

1 Corinthians 2:1-3

[1] And when I came to you, brethren, I did not come with superiority of speech or of wisdom, proclaiming to you the testimony of God. [2] For I determined to know nothing among you except Jesus Christ, and Him crucified. [3] I was with you in weakness and in fear and in much trembling,

1 Corinthians 3:18-19

[18] Let no man deceive himself. If any man among you thinks that he is wise in this age, he must become foolish, so that he may become wise. [19] For the wisdom of this world is foolishness before God.

1 Corinthians 4:10

We are fools for Christ's sake, but you are prudent in Christ; we are weak, but you are strong; you are distinguished, but we are without honor.

Some Christians Proclaim More Than Others. Some Disciple More. GOD Does the Saving.

1 Corinthians 3:6-9

[6] I planted, Apollos watered, but God was causing the growth. [7] So then neither the one who plants nor the one who waters is anything, but God who causes the growth. [8] Now he who plants and he who waters are one; but each will receive his own reward according to his own labor. [9] For we are God's fellow workers; you are God's field, God's building.

GOD Opens Doors and Lead the Way for Gospel Proclamation.

1 Corinthians 16:9
for a wide door for effective *service* has opened to me, and there are many adversaries.

2 Corinthians 2:14
But thanks be to God, who always leads us in triumph in Christ, and manifests through us the sweet aroma of the knowledge of Him in every place.

People Who Reject or Oppose the Gospel Are in Satan's Kingdom and Doing Satan's Work. Pray for Them.

Matthew 12:30
He who is not with Me is against Me; and he who does not gather with Me scatters.

Mark 3:27
But no one can enter the strong man's house [Satan's kingdom] and plunder his property [people who belong to Satan] unless he first binds the strong man [Satan], and then he will plunder his house [by taking back souls for JESUS].

Ephesians 6:12
For we wrestle not against flesh and blood, but against principalities, against powers, against the rulers of the darkness of this world, against spiritual wickedness in high places. (KJV)

We Must Beware of Those Preaching a False "Jesus" and a False "Gospel."

2 Corinthians 11:3-4 & 13-15
[3] But I am afraid that, as the serpent deceived Eve by his craftiness, your minds will be led astray from the simplicity and purity *of devotion* to Christ. [4] For if one comes and preaches another Jesus whom we have not preached, or you receive a different spirit which you have not received, or

a different gospel which you have not accepted, you bear *this* beautifully.

[13] For such men are false apostles, deceitful workers, disguising themselves as apostles of Christ. [14] No wonder, for even Satan disguises himself as an angel of light. [15] Therefore it is not surprising if his servants also disguise themselves as servants of righteousness, whose end will be according to their deeds.

Be Aware That People Can Receive a False "Holy Spirit." We Must Test the Spirits.

(See 1 Corinthians 4:4, listed earlier.)

1 Thessalonians 5:19-21
[19] Do not quench the Spirit; [20] do not despise prophetic utterances. [21] But examine everything *carefully*; hold fast to that which is good; [22] abstain from every form of evil.

1 John 4:1-2
[1] Beloved, do not believe every spirit, but test the spirits to see whether they are from God, because many false prophets have gone out into the world. [2] By this you know the Spirit of God: every spirit that confesses that Jesus Christ has come in the flesh is from God;

Beware of False Church Leaders and False "Christians."

Acts 20:28-30
[28] Be on guard for yourselves and for all the flock, among which the Holy Spirit has made you overseers, to shepherd the church of God which He purchased with His own blood. [29] I know that after my departure savage wolves will come in among you, not sparing the flock; [30] and from among your own selves men will arise, speaking perverse things, to draw away the disciples after them.

Matthew 7:15-16

[15] "Beware of the false prophets, who come to you in sheep's clothing, but inwardly are ravenous wolves. [16] You will know them by their fruits. Grapes are not gathered from thorn *bushes* nor figs from thistles, are they?

Matthew 7: 21-23

[21] "Not everyone who says to Me, 'Lord, Lord,' will enter the kingdom of heaven, but he who does the will of My Father who is in heaven *will enter*. [22] Many will say to Me on that day, 'Lord, Lord, did we not prophesy in Your name, and in Your name cast out demons, and in Your name perform many miracles?' [23] And then I will declare to them, 'I never knew you; DEPART FROM ME, YOU WHO PRACTICE LAWLESSNESS.'

Matthew 24:24-25

[24] For false Christs and false prophets will arise and will show great signs and wonders, so as to mislead, if possible, even the elect. [25] Behold, I have told you in advance.

We Must Care for the Basic Needs of the Poor.

Deuteronomy 15:11

For the poor will never cease *to be* in the land; therefore I command you, saying, 'You shall freely open your hand to your brother, to your needy and poor in your land.'

Psalm 41:1

How blessed is he who considers the helpless; The LORD will deliver him in a day of trouble.

Psalm 72:12

For he will deliver the needy when he cries for help, The afflicted also, and him who has no helper.

Proverbs 14:21

He who despises his neighbor sins,
But happy is he who is gracious to the poor.

-2-
HELPFUL CHARTS

In this chapter, you will find seven helpful charts you can return to for reference. I suggest putting a tab on this page for easy access to these charts.

Gospel Conversation & Evangelism Task Chart
The first chart in this chapter gives you a quick overview of a typical Gospel conversation. The second chart lists out the 21 tasks in this book to help you plan ahead. You might need to acquire materials or switch some of the tasks around to fit your schedule or group needs. Please, do whatever it takes to remain faithful to the completion of all 21 tasks.

Five False Beliefs Charts
As you evangelize, you will encounter many people who follow false religions and hold false beliefs. The five charts on the following pages offer a glance at some of those beliefs and simple truths that expose these beliefs for the traps that they are. We love all people, but we hate the false systems that trap them. The difference between JESUS and all other beliefs is not the difference between water and soft drinks, but water and arsenic. To love others is to warn them if they've been drinking poison. We do this by sharing the Gospel with them. By proclaiming the Gospel, we administer the antidote to Satan's Kool-Aid. Whether or not our neighbors accept the antidote is between them and GOD, but we must do our part. We cannot keep the cure to ourselves, not if we want to stand before GOD blameless on judgment day.

Imagine if I saw that you had been trapped inside a cage with a ravenous lion, and I had the key to let you out, but I didn't attempt to free you. I would not be very loving. In fact, you would think I was murderous and cruel. And you'd be right. Without JESUS, people are trapped inside a cage with Satan who ravenously stalks souls to devour. True love means attempting to release Satan's captives. We must love our atheist, pagan, Muslim, Catholic, Jewish, LDS, Jehovah's Witnesses, and "kindness is king" neighbors enough to offer them the key to their freedom—the cross of JESUS CHRIST.

Key Bible Verses to Combat False Beliefs
Please see the *EVANGELIZE GEORGIA* website for a list of key Bible verses to reference when encountering people trapped in false beliefs. I keep copies of this list one me and hand them out whenever appropriate. I suggest you memorize or have handy a handful of verses that prove JESUS is GOD IN FLESH and CO-CREATOR with the FATHER, that the TRINITY is real, and that JESUS and the FATHER are ONE. A few of my favorites are **Isaiah 9:6, Matthew 28:18-20, John 1:1-3, John 10:30, Colossians 1:15-17, and Hebrews 1:1-4**. To prove we're saved by grace, through faith and not of works, please memorize **Ephesians 2:8-9**.

One Religion to Rule Them All
You will encounter many other false belief systems in addition to the five listed on these charts. These five are probably the most common ones you'll encounter in the United States, baring ethnic pockets, which may have a high concentration of other false religions. All false religions follow the same pattern of false beliefs, just repackaged or put into different terms. At the core of all false beliefs, you will discover Satan's one-world religion, which promotes "kindness" toward all except Jews and Christians, salvation by being a good person, a lack of judgment for sin, antisemitism, the support of Israel's enemies, and tolerance for all beliefs except Christianity.

Many people who are trapped in cults and false religions are oftentimes embarrassed of what their false religion actually teaches and will claim the one-world religion as their own. For example, many Muslims are embarrassed by the fact that Muhammad was a pedophile and that Islam promotes violence as a means to conversion. Such "Muslims" will deny these beliefs of Islam and say something like they believe in "being kind" and "doing good." Such "Muslims" are either lying to you or they're actually religious apostates.

21 DAYS OF EVANGELISM

Gospel Conversation Chart

Initiate the conversation.	My name is ____. I'm out here praying for people today. Can I pray for you? Is there any way I can pray for you today? Would you bless me by letting me pray for you today? What's your name?	
	YES	**NO/ I'M GOOD**
Determine the person's beliefs.	When I pray, I pray in the name of JESUS. Do you know JESUS? Have you committed to JESUS? Have you been reborn by the blood of JESUS? Are you a new creature in JESUS? Has your life been completely transformed by JESUS?	What's the hesitation? Would you like to know how to be great? What's your spiritual background? Has anyone ever told you about how JESUS died for your sins on the cross? It's healthy to talk about our differences. It shows we're open-minded.
Probe for Gospel knowledge.	How would you explain to someone how to get to Heaven?	I'm going to bless you by sharing how JESUS can make you brand new. (Or maybe share a small snippet about how you were lost before JESUS.)
Share the Gospel.	Explain the Gospel (death, burial, resurrection of JESUS). Explain the outcome of our beliefs: Forgiveness of sin and eternity in Heaven vs trapped in sin and Hell bound.	If the person is still with you, share the Gospel of JESUS and Heaven/Hell. Don't worry if people walk off offended. Pray for those who reject JESUS.
The Call to Commit	Would You like to receive GOD's free gift of eternal life in CHRIST JESUS right now? Would you like to be reborn in JESUS today? Would you like to be transformed by JESUS today?	If the person is still with you, call her to commit to JESUS. See box to the left.
	YES	**NO**
Certificate of Rebirth	Go over Certificate of Rebirth if you have one with you. Try taping a copy to a clipboard for reference. See *EG* website for certificate.	See questions and comments below.
Prayer of Commitment	Present the person to GOD as HIS new child in JESUS CHRIST. Thank JESUS for HIS blood. Ask JESUS to baptize the person with the Holy Spirit, to seal the person for the resurrection. Ask the HOLY SPIRIT to help the person overcome any sin and to walk with JESUS. Leave silence for the person to pray. Have her repeat a sinner's prayer after you. Encourage her to thank JESUS.	What's the hesitation? Is there a sin you don't want to give up? Is it family pressure? Do you struggle with pride? Make sure the person understands Hell is eternal torment. It is all pain and anguish without a drop of relief. Also, make sure the person understands she will face GOD alone at the judgment. It won't matter what her family believes.
Parting ways	Encourage the person to give up sin, find Christian fellowship, read the Bible daily, pray without ceasing, get baptized. Give her any tracts, Christian literature, or Bibles you can. Exchange contact information if you feel led.	Encourage the person to think about JESUS more, to read the Bible and Gospel tracts. Send her away with any Christian literature you can.

***As the HOLY SPIRIT leads, heal people and cast out demons in the name of JESUS.

21-Days of Evangelism – Task Chart

DAY 1 Change your email signature and social media status to show you're on team JESUS. ALSO, ask your church to put you on the prayer list because you'll be evangelizing.	DAY 2 Text or email an unbelieving friend or family member. Include **John 3:16-18** or a Gospel tract with your message.	DAY 3 Order, buy, or make a JESUS t-shirt. If you own one already, get it out and resolve to wear it the next time you go out in public, especially on days when evangelizing.
DAY 4 Do a prayer walk or drive through your neighborhood.	DAY 5 Order or make a JESUS yard sign. You might also opt for JESUS car magnets and/or a bumper sticker.	DAY 6 Buy at least 4 cheap Bibles to giveaway. New Testaments or Gospels of John are fine.
DAY 7 Put 3 Bibles in your neighborhood "My Little Library," or one nearby, or give the Bibles to people you see walking around.	DAY 8 Read sample Gospel tracts and brainstorm how you would make your own tract.	DAY 9 Draft your own Gospel tract.
DAY 10 Edit your tract. Let it sit for a few days. Plan to print it on Day 13.	DAY 11 Prepare a small gift and plan to give the gift and tract to a neighbor on Day 14.	DAY 12 Practice explaining the Gospel of JESUS CHRIST out loud.
DAY 13 Edit your tract one last time. Print it. Optional: Make many copies.	DAY 14 Give your tract and gift to a neighbor.	DAY 15 Do a prayer walk or drive through a poor neighborhood.
DAY 16 Make a blessing bag or buy a meal gift card to give away on Day 17.	DAY 17 Give a blessing bag or meal card to someone who is homeless or needy.	DAY 18 Cut out, copy, or print 3 Gospel tracts.
DAY 19 Give out 3 tracts or Gospel goodie bags for employee appreciation around your town, or leave the goodies as doorhangers in a poor neighborhood.	DAY 20 Print or make a FREE PRAYER sign.	DAY 21 Carry a FREE PRAYER sign around in public and pray with people in JESUS' name. Share the Gospel as the SPIRIT leads.

Muslim

False Beliefs	Truths
Many are uninformed or ashamed of actual Muslim beliefs. Some claim to be Muslim, but actually follow a "be kind" one-world false religion. Allah is "God." JESUS didn't die on cross. Good deeds outweigh bad. JESUS was a prophet, but Muhammad is Allah's prophet. Deny GOD has a SON Say the TRINITY is polytheism Might ask you to not pray in JESUS' name because it offends them May not realize the Koran tells Muslims to hate Jews and Christians (People of the Book). See sura 5 and many other passages. May not realize the prophet Muhammad was a pedophile Are waiting for the appearing of the Mahdi in an event that counterfeits JESUS's return Think Koran predates Bible and is the true "holy book." Say Koran is superior because only one version exists and will try to deny that there were many variations of the Koran until Uthman ibn Affan had all but one version destroyed.	It sounds like you believe in good works (or "kindness") and not what the Koran actually teaches. The GOD of the Bible is the one true GOD, not Allah. JESUS is GOD's SON. JESUS is GOD IN FLESH. JESUS is THE suffering PROPHET whose bodily death on the cross paid for our sins. JESUS is supreme. HE will return as KING OF KINGS AND LORD OF LORDS. We're saved by grace through faith. The TRINITY is ONE GOD in three persons, not three separate "gods." Definitely pray in JESUS' name. Another person can't force you to speak or not speak in a certain way. One of Muhammad's 12 wives, Aisha, was 6 or 7 at time of marriage and 9 at consummation. JESUS is perfect. HE never lusted after a single woman, though He was tempted in every way. Dead Sea Scroll discoveries confirm Bible predates Koran by a landslide. Koran was written around 610 and was recited to the false prophet Muhammad by demon claiming to be the Angel Gabriel. The Koran says the Bible is true. If the Bible is true, then the Koran must be false.

21 DAYS OF EVANGELISM

Latter Day Saints (LDS/Mormon)

False Beliefs	Truths
Will claim to be Christian, will agree with the Gospel, will even tell you JESUS is the SON OF GOD	Why are you trying so hard to convince me you're a Christian? Aren't you proud of the LDS church?
Believe the Bible but accept Joseph Smith's *Book of Mormon* as their authority even though it wasn't published until 1830	JESUS always existed as GOD and was born as GOD IN FLESH. HE is CO-CREATOR with the FATHER. JESUS created Satan. JESUS and Satan are not both "sons of GOD." JESUS is the SON.
LDS churches are led by false apostles and prophets, such as Joseph Smith, who was an adulterer and preyed on teenage girls.	Do you think GOD is going to allow a council of men to ruin HIS word? The books of the cannon were selected because of their mathematical perfection, among other reasons, that prove they are inerrant scripture.
Believe the Cannon is corrupt because a council of men chose the books that have been included	It's fine to read books outside of the Cannon, especially the books that almost made it into the cannon, but only the 66 books of the Bible should be accepted as GOD's perfect and authoritative word.
Believe Satan and JESUS are brothers, that both are sons of GOD.	
Believe that there are many sons of GOD	
Say JESUS was born a man but worked his way up to divine	Joseph Smith was just a man, but you value his writings above GOD's. Many of Smith's prophecies failed to come true, and he was an adulterer. JESUS never sinned once.
Believe faith in the Gospel plus good works saves	
Don't believe Hell is eternal.	GOD condemns anyone who adds to the Bible.
In the afterlife, men become gods and create their own galaxies. Women become goddesses and make babies for eternity.	We're saved by grace, through faith in CHRIST alone.
LDS church teaches doctrine of polygamy, but supposedly don't encourage practicing it any longer.	Hell is eternal torment in the Lake of Fire.

21 DAYS OF EVANGELISM

Jehovah's Witnesses

False Beliefs	Truths
Claim to be Christian and will tell you they believe the Gospel Jehovah is the only true "God." JESUS is SON OF GOD, but HE's not part of the trinity. Deny JESUS is creator Deny the trinity Believe JESUS is "a god" Say JESUS was Archangel Michael before HIS birth Follow a corrupted translation of the Bible called the New World Translation. One of the most heretical edits of this translation can be found in **John 1:1**. The translators changed the phrase "He [JESUS] was God" to "He [JESUS] was *a* god." JWs used to teach that only 144,000 Jehovah's Witnesses get to Heaven and reign with Christ. Had to change that statement as the cult grew. Hell is a place of unconsciousness or non-existence. Will tell you they don't judge different beliefs and would never tell anyone a different belief could result in going to Hell. Think JESUS invisibly returned to Earth in 1914 and is now enthroned as King in Heaven	If JESUS is "a god," but you claim Jehovah is the only GOD, then your Bible must be corrupt. To say that JESUS is "a god" implies there are many gods'. JESUS is GOD IN FLESH. All things were created by and through HIM. JESUS is co-creator with THE FATHER and HOLY SPIRIT. The TRINITY is real. The Bible does not use the word "trinity" but the concept is clearly communicated throughout all of scripture. Anyone who is a new creation in JESUS enters Heaven. Hell is a place of eternal torment in the Lake of Fire. GOD gives us the ability to make judgments about different beliefs, to discern truth from lies. Either you don't actually believe the JW religion is the only way to Heaven, or you don't love others enough to warn them they won't make it to Heaven unless they follow the JW religion. JESUS' return to Earth will be visible and undeniable to everyone. JESUS' physical rule from Jerusalem as KING OF KINGS AND LORD OF LORDS will be known by all.

21 DAYS OF EVANGELISM

Catholic

False Beliefs	Truths
Believe you're saved by partaking of the seven sacraments (Baptism, Confirmation, Eucharist, Penance, and Reconciliation, Anointing the Sick, Holy Orders, and Matrimony) Believe sins are forgiven by confessing them to a priest Believe in being a good person, that good deeds can outweigh the bad Many Catholics believe you must be Catholic to go to Heaven. Pray to Mary and the saints Bow to religious idols and use rosary beads during prayer Believe Pope is the head of the church Believe JESUS died on the cross but don't realize they need to accept HIM personally for forgiveness of sin	We're saved by grace, through faith in CHRIST alone. Being a "good person" can never make you a new person. JESUS tells us we must be born again if we're going to enter HIS Kingdom (**John 3:3**). We pray to GOD directly because JESUS tore the curtain to the Holy of Holies through HIS death on the cross. We do not need Mary, saints, idols, or priests to reach GOD. GOD alone forgives sins through the blood of JESUS. No human or priest can forgive our sins. We confess our sins directly to GOD in JESUS' name. JESUS is the head of the church (**Colossians 1:18**). Many Catholics come to faith in JESUS upon hearing the Gospel. Praise GOD!!!

Jewish

Partial Truths	Truths
Believe in the Hebrew Bible, which Christians call the Old Testament. Reject the New Testament. Still waiting for MESSIAH to come the first time Believe MESSIAH will literally come to Jerusalem and inhabit the third temple they're trying to rebuild, not realizing this will be the temple the Anti-Christ desecrates Reject JESUS of Nazareth is the Jewish MESSIAH and the SAVIOR OF THE WORLD Many think believing in JESUS means they have to give up being Jewish. Many Jewish people today are secular and don't know or practice Judaism. They tend to hold mystic or New Age beliefs or they believe in "kindness" as they way to GOD.	JESUS of Nazareth is the Jewish MESSIAH and the SAVIOR OF THE WORLD. JESUS is Jewish. You can be Jewish and believe in JESUS. Christians also believe MESSIAH will literally return to Jerusalem, but Christians understand JESUS is MESSIAH. Many Jewish people reject JESUS as MESSIAH and will, thereby, accept the Anti-Christ as MESSIAH. Only the true MESSIAH, JESUS, will be able to save Israel, which HE will do when they repent and cry. "Maranatha, LORD JESUS." JESUS fulfilled many prophecies of the Bible at HIS first coming, about 2000 years ago, the most significant of these being HIS sacrifice on the cross as GOD's perfect Passover lamb. JESUS paid for the sins of the world when HE died on the cross. HE was buried and resurrected immortal on the third day. See Isaiah 53 and Psalm 22, among other passages. Jews and Gentiles alike must trust that the perfect blood of JESUS has paid for sin and that JESUS is the only way to receive eternal life with GOD. JESUS will fulfill all the other prophecies in the Hebrew Bible at HIS second coming. HE will save Israel, restore the Jewish people to the promised land, and HE will rule out of Jerusalem as KING OF KINGS AND LORD OF LORDS.

-3-
Prepare Yourself For Evangelism.

In this chapter, I share how you can prepare yourself for evangelism through devotion to GOD and the recognition of the enemy's lies and tactics to get you to stop evangelizing. I also offer several plain truths all Christians need to understand as they do the work of an evangelist.

Study to Show Yourself Approved for GOD's Work.

Spend Time With JESUS Daily.
In Acts 4, the Jewish rulers recognized that Peter and John had been with JESUS because of their confident speech and the power of the HOLY SPIRIT working through them. If we want this same confidence and power as we minister the Gospel, then we must do as Peter and John did and spend time with JESUS. We must pray continually, read the Bible daily, fellowship with other Christians, and memorize scripture. I will elaborate more on personal development in Chapter 4 when I address putting on the full armor of GOD.

Pray Specifically for Evangelism.
Fast and pray for specific evangelism outings, certain locations GOD puts on your heart, salvation for others, protection of your body and reputation when evangelizing, good weather, and open doors for the Gospel. As you evangelize, write down the names of the people you meet in a notebook, and pray over 1-2 columns of names each day. See the video on how to pray on the *EVANGELIZE GEORGIA* YouTube channel: https://www.youtube.com/watch?v=iVY070n-_pw&t=192s

Make Quiet Time Quiet.
For best results with Bible reading and prayer, I recommend finding a quiet place and using 34DB ear muffs to block out noises. Even if my house is quiet, I find the earmuffs help me to focus better. Earplugs work,

21 DAYS OF EVANGELISM

as well, but are more difficult to keep up with. If you use an electronic headset, make sure not to play any media while studying the Bible and praying. White noise should be okay if you like that kind of thing.

If you haven't been reading the Bible regularly, please start now. Read a chapter each day from the Gospel of John. You'll be done in 21 days. Or read the chapter from Proverbs that corresponds to the day of the month. There are 31 chapters in Proverbs. For a challenge, read both a chapter from John and Proverbs each day. Consider adding a Psalm as well.

A Word About That Scary Word, "Fasting"
As per fasting, you can give up solid food for a set number of days, or half days, as long as you're healthy and able. I like to fast for the same number of days as an upcoming event. For example, if I have a two-day evangelism event, I will fast for two days or two half days. Half-day fasting basically means I skip breakfast or lunch or both.

See the video and guide to fasting on the *EVANGELIZE GEORGIA* website at https://evangelizegeorgia.org/free-guide-to-fasting/.Or research your desired fast of choice. Many Christians have done the Daniel Fast, and there are many other kind of fasts out there.

Instead of fasting from food, or in addition to fasting from food, you can also try fasting from certain pleasures, like sweets, eating out, entertainment, your phone, video games, movies and shows, social media, and the internet.

Study Other Evangelists.
One of the greatest benefits of living in times such as these is the ability to watch seasoned evangelists engage in Gospel conversations without having to leave the house. I highly encourage you to take a little time each day to watch a video, or listen to the audio, of street evangelists and preachers sharing the Gospel in public.
- **Ray Comfort** - Living Waters - *Just Witnessing* is a channel of Ray Comfort's street evangelism videos: https://www.youtube.com/@raycomfortjustwitnessing
- **Cliffe Knechtle** – *Give Me an Answer* https://www.youtube.com/@askcliffe
- **Pastor David Jonathan Lynn** -

Christ's Forgiveness Ministries
https://www.youtube.com/@christsforgiveness
- **Nicholas Bowling** - *Nicholas Bowling*
  https://www.youtube.com/@NicholasBowling
- **Phillip Blair** - *Torch of Christ Ministries*
  https://www.youtube.com/@TorchofChristMinistries

Know Your Enemies.

Another way to prepare for evangelism is to understand the forces that will oppose you. In addition to attacks from Satan, your own flesh, and this dark and depraved world, you will also (surprisingly) encounter opposition from other Christians, and even well-respected church leaders.

Pray for your enemies, especially the ones who hinder GOD'S work. Many of the Christians who fall into this category of hindering GOD's work are blind to their own misconceptions, and we must reprove, rebuke, and exhort them with great patience and instruction (**2 Timothy 4:2**). Remember that you too were once blind to the things of GOD. We were all HIS enemies before we understood HIS grace and JESUS saved us. We all, at some point in our lives, opposed the work of GOD—either by mocking those doing it, or by simply not doing it.

Common Attacks From Your Own Flesh

When it comes time to evangelize, you will discover, that second to Satan, you are your own worst enemy. Any excuse to not evangelize or to delay evangelizing, such as feeling ill-equipped or alone, is from your own flesh. Any fear is your greatest enemy, which is why JESUS ends HIS Great Commission with words of assurance that HE will be with us always (**Matthew 28:20**). The implied command is to not be afraid.

The following sections of this book expose common lies and traps you will be tempted indulge as you go and evangelize.

The Lie That You're Untrained
You don't need training before evangelizing. JESUS will train you as you go. JESUS said to follow HIM to learn how to make fishers of men

(**Matthew 4:19**). He didn't say take a course, read a book, take a personality test, get session approval, form a committee, get your church on board, and then maybe if everything checks out, try fishing for men. You don't even need to read this book before you evangelize! Seek first the Kingdom of GOD. Go and complete the one task JESUS has given to HIS followers—recruiting Kingdom subjects on HIS behalf. All the training and support will follow.

You don't learn a sport by studying it. You learn by playing. The same principle applies with evangelism. There may come a time for you to take courses and read books, but if you want to learn how to evangelize, you must start by getting out there and playing ball.

The Lie That Evangelism Is Only For Some Christians
Evangelism isn't a gifting for some Christians, it's a calling for all. There are a variety of ways Christians can engage in evangelism. There is a part to be played for each member of the body when it comes to getting the Gospel out into the world.

The gifting of evangelism in Ephesians 4 is referring to the office of a leading Evangelist. An Evangelist who leads others in evangelism is a gift to a local church body. Sadly, many churches have neglected evangelism, and very few of them have the gift of a leading evangelist in their midst.

We Doubt the Truth That in Our Weakness HE is Strong.
JESUS promises that power is perfected in weakness (**2 Corinthians 12:9**). HE shines brightest through our lack of gifting and skill. If you think you are the worst person for evangelism, then GOD can do HIS most mighty work through you. All you have to do is go in faith. If you are lacking in anything, GOD will provide it as you do HIS work. The CHIEF SHEPHERD never leaves HIS sheep in want (**Psalm 23:1**). It gives GOD great pleasure and glory to use the despised things of the world for HIS Kingdom work (**1 Corinthians 1:28**).

The Lie That New and Young Christians Can't Evangelize
Even Children and new believers can evangelize or learn how as they shadow other believers.

The Woman at the Well, for example, had no evangelism training outside of her personal testimony, and she bore witness of JESUS to her entire village (**John 4:7-44**). Also, Samaritans only had access to the first five books of the Bible. Most Christians have access to all 66 books. What better training manual can we possess than the entire cannon of scripture? We are without excuse!

If you need another example of someone who had no training before he went evangelizing, please read **Mark 5:1-20**, in which JESUS commands the man formerly known as Legion to evangelize HIS village almost immediately following his conversion. This man, who knew very little outside of a life of demon possession, went on to evangelize in Decapolis (**Mark 5:20**).

The Personality Test Excuse

The results of your personality test are never an excuse to not share the Gospel. Pinpointing your personality type and then trying to foretell what kind of work GOD has for you is a prime example of consulting something other than GOD for wisdom. Quite frankly, it verges on sorcery. This might sound harsh to some, but I'm not writing this book to tickle ears. The results of these tests are questionable, at best, and the very act of taking them causes us to deviate from JESUS' plain and simple command to take Gospel to the ends of the earth in faith.

Even if a respected church leader tells you a certain personality test is based on the Bible, I highly encourage you to refuse it. Instead of wasting your time on these useless exercises, read the Bible and believe GOD when HE says you can't please HIM without faith (**Hebrews 11:6**). HIS grace is sufficient (**2 Corinthians 12:9**). Remember, we walk by faith, not by the results of a manmade personality test (**2 Corinthians 5:7**). GOD guides our steps, not our own personal assessment of the gifts and talents we think we possess.

Personal Note: I have been known to throw away personality tests, right there, in the middle of Bible study. I attend Bible study to study the Bible. Period.

The Lie That You Need Permission or Approval to Evangelize

You don't need human permission to follow God's Great Commission. **Matthew 28:18-20** is your divine permission slip from JESUS. Go in faith, and fight the urge to seek approval from others when getting started. There might come times when you need human permission to set up an evangelism tent at a certain event or location, but you don't need a human to tell you that you may start evangelizing. GOD has already spoken. Arise and go!

Attacks From Family, Fellow Christians, and Church Leaders

The Enemy in Your Home

Your own family and close friends will most likely mock you for evangelizing, even if they are churchgoing "Christians." If the people closest to you are not in the habit of evangelizing, the HOLY SPIRIT will convict them when they see you doing it. There are two possible reactions to the conviction of the HOLY SPIRIT—disobedience or obedience. Stay faithful to evangelism, and some of your mockers might join you one day. But don't be surprised if some of your besties persistently mock you.

Your Local Church Might Even Oppose You.

Some Christians will try to delay or stop your evangelism by suggesting you need session approval, that you shouldn't do anything apart from church supervision, that you need to read a certain book or take a certain class, or that you need some kind of human approval or certification before you can go and be obedient to GOD.

Other Christians will take jabs at your efforts by criticizing you for not making more disciples. Your own dear church friends might even complain about not seeing people being baptized from your evangelism. Yes, the end goal of evangelism is to baptize and raise up others to go and evangelize, but we can't reach the end goal if we never begin with step 1, which is to go and proclaim the Gospel in faith.

Moreover, one plants, another waters, and GOD is the one who grows up the believers (**1 Corinthians 3:6-7**). The people who make complaints about a lack of disciples being made need to air their grievances with GOD, since HE is the ONE responsible for the results. Plus, you are only one person. You can either focus on planting the seeds or watering them. Sure, one person can attempt to do both, as I have tried to do before, but it is best to have another person to help with follow up and discipleship. I always invite my "discipleship critics" to help me with evangelism follow up, but I rarely get a taker.

Also, we live in the days of Noah. Just as Noah had zero converts outside of his family, you might not see the fruit you'd like to see from your efforts right away, or on this side of life. JESUS' Great Commission remains the same, regardless of the results. We are to proclaim the Gospel whenever we can, not to proclaim it only if we see tangible results. And I guarantee you will eventually see results because GOD guarantees results (**Galatians 6:9**). The Gospel is the very power of GOD (**Romans 1:16**). GOD's word never returns void (**Isaiah 55:11**). It might take some time before you see people making decisions for JESUS, but it will happen. Don't grow weary. Endure.

Be encouraged, as you evangelize more, you will learn to listen to the HOLY SPIRIT better. HE will lead you to the people who need to hear the Gospel the most. For example, you might go on an evangelism outing thinking you're going to witness to a certain group of people at an event, but then the SPIRIT leads you to a janitor or a cook who you didn't expect was listening and searching for JESUS. The opportunities abound when you follow GOD's heartbeat.

Compromised Christians Will Oppose the Gospel.
Compromised, weak, or false Christians will try to silence or hinder evangelism by giving you worldly "wisdom" about being more diplomatic, more sophisticated, more academic, more socially acceptable, and less bold. Such Christians will oftentimes try to anesthetize the Gospel by telling you to focus on the love of GOD and not to talk about Hell or to present Hell as merely "separation" from GOD.

The Bible is clear that Hell is eternal torment in the Lake of Fire. GOD created Hell to torment Satan and the fallen demons (**Matthew 25:41**). Just imagine how bad of a place it must be. Not warning people about the reality of such a horrible place is downright cruel.

And to be clear, GOD is present in Hell because GOD is omnipresent. The Book of Revelation tells us that people and demons in Hell are tortured in JESUS' presence (**Revelation 14:10-11**). The "separation" from GOD that people experience in Hell is more accurately described as separation from HIS countenance or blessings. (Please study the original Greek for **2 Thessalonians 1:9.**) Hell is the full presence of GOD's wrath and justice, without a drop of blessing or mercy.

Think about the thirstiest you've ever been. Multiply that desperation for a drink by a million. Now imagine you're trapped in a fiery hot furnace where you will never ever ever find drinkable water. That's just a small hint of what Hell will be like. Hell is so horrifying that GOD wishes not a single human would perish there (**2 Peter 3:9**). He sent HIS own SON to save humans from having to go there.

No one is doing anyone any favors by editing the Gospel, which is the good news of JESUS saving us from sin and eternal death in Hell. If you sugarcoat or ignore the topic of Hell, you will only hurt yourself because you're subtracting from GOD's word, making yourself an editor, rather than a faithful proclaimer, of HIS message of salvation. GOD have mercy on your soul.

Compromised or False Christians Will Accuse Obedient Christians of "Giving Christianity a Bad Name."
As you evangelize according to GOD's model, some professing Christians will criticize you, or people like you, such as street preachers, by saying something to the effect of "You're giving Christians a bad name." Such people will suggest that you subdue your evangelism and make it more "friendly," "inviting," and "loving." Such suggestions are veiled accusations against you. What these professing Christians are actually doing is accusing you of being obnoxious, unfriendly, offensive, and hateful.

Such criticism of Biblical evangelism is from Satan. Satan can always use unbelievers to make accusations against Bible-obedient Christians, but he especially loves it when he can get a professing Christian to do his dirty work. It's more cutting when your fellow churchgoer, as opposed to a random warlock on the street, says something that could potentially make you feel like a criminal for evangelizing according to

GOD's model. Hold up your shield of faith, and extinguish these comments immediately. Then, pray for the people who make such comments. We want to see them repent and join you in true evangelism.

Some "Evangelistic" Ministries Hurt Evangelism.

Some very large "evangelistic" organizations will "re-think" or "redefine" evangelism to make it more subdued, refined, seeker friendly, scholarly, and socially acceptable. They will encourage Christians to build bridges with the world. They will suggest putting the Gospel of JESUS at the tail end, rather than at the head, of ministry events. For example, they will encourage Christians to run courses and host dinners in order to ease people into a Gospel discussions *later*. Courses and dinners are great for growing disciples, reducing evangelism to a course eliminates GOD's command to go in faith and confines Gospel ministry to a classroom or dinner table.

By the grace of GOD, people can still get saved through courses and fellowship dinners, but the people and churches running these events lose the opportunity to serve GOD according to HIS ministry model. Don't fall for these cosmopolitan "evangelistic" models of ministry. Any human or organization who dares to puff up, complicate, or "redefine" GOD's Great Commission is in error, no matter how big and influential his or her organization may be.

Our prayer is that the people behind these false ministry models would repent and follow GOD's pure and simple model for Gospel proclamation as given in the Bible. No one has perfect theology. We care about these ministers who are deceived into thinking they can redefine a concept GOD has already defined, and we want to see them in Heaven too. Imagine if these compromised organizations did repent—what a great Gospel revival that could spark!

JESUS, and later the Apostles, always led ministry with Kingdom proclamation and miracles, wherever they went. They never hosted events or programs with the hopes of *later* sharing the Gospel with attendees. JESUS never put on a dinner party to make sinners feel comfortable with their sin before easing into a lecture about repentance. In fact, JESUS made dinner parties uncomfortable (**Luke 7 and 11**). HE did not flatter, disarm, or make accommodations for the sinners with whom HE dined. HE directly attacked sin. Those who were humble of heart received HIS correction and looked to HIM for salvation. The proud sinners were offended and remained offended.

People are either going to accept or reject JESUS, no matter how disarming and lovely your dinner or program may be. And you certainly don't want to risk making your church events so worldly that unbelievers feel comfortable remaining in their unbelief. In fact, if you're church is healthy, unbelievers should be convicted of their sin and either storm out feeling offended or remain and be transformed by the Gospel. To be clear unbelievers who reject JESUS should feel uncomfortable at your church, not because of mistreatment or disrespect, but because the conviction of the HOLY SPIRIT is so strong they can't stand to be there. Do as JESUS did. Share the Gospel and disciple the folks who receive THE LORD and stick around. Stop pandering to the worldly-minded.

Fearful Christians Add Burdens to Evangelism.
Compromised Christians, weak Christians, or false Christians will give you evangelism "advice" that complicates and adds burdens to the very simple task of proclaiming JESUS. For these Christians, the Gospel just isn't powerful enough on its own, despite GOD's emphatic statements that the Gospel is the power of GOD to save anyone who believes (**Romans 1:16, 1 Corinthians 1:18**). Beware of such people, who have a form of godliness but deny the very power of GOD (**2 Timothy 3:5**). Lovingly speak truth to such brothers and sisters, all the while praying JESUS will free them from the Satanic Spirit of timidity. It might take some time, but a few of these fearful Christians might repent and come evangelizing with you.

Fearful and compromised Christians will also confuse acts of kindness with evangelism. They will tell you to show the love of CHRIST by doing kind things for others instead of talking about the cross. Sadly, this bad advice is a result of poor preaching in the churches today. Many church leaders falsely teach their sheep that people need to see JESUS in our acts of kindness before they can hear about HIM. This is the exact opposite of what GOD tells us in the Bible.

JESUS takes first place in all we do. HE is the head of the church and has supremacy in all we do (**Colossians 1:18**). The greatest love JESUS showed us is the cross, and the greatest love a person can show to another is sharing the cross. People must encounter the power of GOD through the preaching of the Gospel, first and foremost. Acts of kindness are great and should be done, but we must keep our priorities in line with GOD's priorities. Preach JESUS first.

Attacks from Unbelievers (Satan's Workers of Iniquity)

People Who Accuse You Are Doing Satan's Work of Criminalizing Evangelism. Accusations Are Demons Speaking.

Satan is the accuser of the brethren, and he will accuse you constantly through others as you evangelize. He will attack your appearances, your family, the way you raise your family, your level of Bible knowledge, your lack of fasting, the authenticity of your salvation, the way you evangelize…the list goes on. Some of Satan's favorite adjectives to use against Christians are *judgmental, hypocritical, controlling, bigoted, black and white, prude, manipulative, legalistic, strict, pushy, close-minded, inflammatory, confrontational, offensive, uneducated, simple-minded, primitive, old-fashioned, rigid, self-righteous, unaccepting, mean, square, conservative*…Yes, Christians are conservative, but when others use the word against us, they mean it in a bad way.

I have even encountered people who will accuse Christians of being *scary* and *dangerous*. These people will clutch their children to "protect" them from the *scary evangelist* who wants to share about how JESUS is the way to Heaven. These people will say something like, "I'm here to spend time with my family," thereby, accusing you of ruining their family time. These very same parents will take their children trick-or-treating to houses with grotesque displays of graveyards and severed limbs in a witch's cauldron. They will take their children to libraries that allow sexually confused people to preach a Satanic Gospel to their precious little one.

Such parents fail to see the difference between spiritual nourishment and spiritual abuse and will offer up their children to Baal while "protecting" them from the Christians who actually care about their souls. If these parents loved their children as much as they claim, they would educate them about how they can be saved from sin and Heaven-bound in JESUS. Pray for such parents and for their children.

One of Satan's most popular accusations to make is that Christians are *pushy*. If you want to see what true religious pushiness or force looks like, please visit the *Voice of the Martyrs* website and read the articles about our dear brothers and sisters who are maimed, killed, imprisoned, kicked out of their own homes, robbed of their livelihoods, and whose houses and churches are burned down because they follow JESUS and not one of the false religions being *pushed* on them.

True Christians would never dream of doing any of these horrible things to get someone to convert to GOD's ways, and if someone claiming to be a Christian does use extreme shunning and violence to make converts, that person is worshipping a false god, not the actual Christian GOD of the Bible.

It is not *pushy* or *forceful* to continually talk to unbelieving friends about JESUS because you care about their souls. It's not *force* to require a child, even a grown child living in your home, to go to church with you because you love that child and want what's best for him. It's not *force* to warn people about the reality of Hell. Accusations against true Christians *forcing* people to accept JESUS are Satanic lies. Demons will use Satan's pawns to accuse you of anything in an attempt to make you stop talking to others about JESUS.

Be informed: When a person tells you not to push your beliefs, she is actually pushing her belief that people should remain silent about GOD. This person believes it's good to censor speech and that she has the authority to bully others into silence. Such a person thinks she has the right to strip you of your inalienable, GOD-given right to free speech. Who, then, is the actual oppressor of the conversation?

Shake the Dust Off Your Feet.
JESUS gives us authority over Satan's kingdom but not over the human will. It is, therefore, a waste of time to keep evangelizing a person who keeps rejecting GOD's free gift of eternal life multiple times. You cannot change this person's will. This person must humble herself before GOD. As the HOLY SPIRIT leads, you may want to move on from evangelizing such a person. By all means, continue to pray for her.

Personal Note: In some cases of spiritual hardness, I have followed the SPIRIT's leading to press into the conversation and keep contending with the person. In these cases, I am sometimes able to get the person to pray with me. I will ask JESUS to unblind such a person so he or she can see the light of the Gospel. Some of these conversations result in the person receiving JESUS. All glory to GOD! On the other hand, don't be surprised if a hardened person turns on you and calls you *pushy* or escalate her complaints against you in some way. Please listen to the HOLY SPIRIT in each and every case.

Kindness Towards "All" Excludes Christians.

The people who believe most strongly in "kindness" as their religion will oftentimes treat true Christians unkindly by mocking and shunning them, destroying Christian items and literature, and making accusations against Christians, churches, and Christianity in general. Such people will say things like they believe in "love" above all else while condemning and shunning Christians. Such people will sometimes, very unkindly, accuse Christians of hypocrisy, failing to see the hypocrisy in their own lives. These people have been taken captive by Satan and need our prayers. JESUS is above all and can set them free!

Hardened Unbelievers Are Captives of Satan and Will Be Your Strongest Opposers. Pray for Them!

People in hardened unbelief will most likely treat you the harshest. Such people include those who are proud to be atheists, proud to be immoral, proud hedonists, leaders of apostate churches, professing "Christians" who believe a false gospel, Satanists, practitioners of witchcraft, or those heavily involved in a cult or false religion. These people have been blinded to the Gospel light by Satan.

Many of these folks will twist scripture to oppose you, just as Satan twisted scripture in his temptation of CHRIST in the wilderness (**Matthew 4:1-11, Luke 4:1-13**). Some of their favorite passages to twist are those about not judging others. Warning people about the dangers of Hell is not the same action as making a judgment to send them to Hell. There is only one JUDGE who has the power over a person's eternal fate, and HIS judgments are perfectly just. The act of warning people about Hell is actually an act of love, not judgment.

Plus, all humans make judgments all day every day. Each of us must constantly judge the world around us for our survival. In this sense, it's myopic to apply the term *judgmental* to Christians alone. A demon-influenced person may go so far as to quote scripture in an attempt to accuse Christians of judging others. Please understand that such a person is doing as her father Satan does. Satan knows the Bible better than anyone. Just because a person is educated in the Bible or can quote a few verses out of context doesn't mean he or she has been born again of GOD. It usually means the exact opposite.

The most hardened of unbelievers will threaten you and, in some cases, report your presence as a problem to the authorities. Don't be intimidated by this bullying. Understand that these accusations are coming from demons, and rejoice when such persecution comes to you because it means you're a big enough threat to cause Satan to raise up his workers of iniquity to come against you. Keep evangelizing. Hold up your shield of faith and remember that HE who is in you is greater than HE who is in the world (**1 John 4:4**). Speak up for JESUS until you take your last breath. Pray and fast for these workers of iniquity, that they will repent and get saved. JESUS is infinitely stronger than Satan and can unblind and save anyone—even the hardest of unbelievers.

Be informed: No one is allowed to touch you, spit at you, throw anything at you, launch or spray anything at you, or touch any of your belongings. If a person touches you, launches anything at you, or attempts to physically harm you, he or she can be charged with assault. If anyone tries to remove any of your belongings from the scene, or from your hands, he or she can be charged with theft or attempted theft. If things get heated while you're ministering the Gospel, you have every right to command people to back away, not touch you, or to get their hands off your stuff. Kindly inform the troublemaker(s) that he or she can be arrested should the harassment continue. Feel free to call the authorities to the scene. Many street ministers video record all their events as an added layer of security. You can look up a GoPro setup or other ways to record your evangelism online.

Plain Vanilla Truths About Evangelism

You Can't Evangelize Effectively Without JESUS.

Both Satan and your own flesh hate evangelism. Satan hates anything that threatens his kingdom, which is exactly what happens whenever the Gospel is proclaimed. And your flesh hates the idea of walking up to people and telling them about JESUS. It seems rude and crude. Your flesh would much rather complicate, puff up, and altogether ignore GOD's pure and simple command to go and proclaim the Gospel. Worry not, JESUS has overcome your sin, Satan, and the world, so you can rebuke your fears, doubts, and opposition in the name of JESUS. Evangelize with JESUS, and walk in HIS victory over Satan, fear, and death (**1 Corinthians 15:57**). Listen to the HOLY SPIRIT every step of the way. Pray continually in the name of JESUS, for this is GOD's will for you (**1 Thessalonians 5:16-17**).

The Gospel Is What Saves Souls.
I've stated this already, but the point is so important it bears repeating. The Gospel saves souls, not your example, your charity, your ministry, your personality, your church... We should pursue excellence in all areas of life, but we must remember—only the Gospel of JESUS CHRIST can bring a dead soul to life.

The Power of the Press Is Powerful Indeed.
People get saved reading the Bible for themselves because the word of GOD is active and alive (**Hebrews 4:12**)! Give away as many Bibles as you can. People also get saved reading Gospel tracts. While spoken word is oftentimes the most effective way to share the Gospel, don't ever underestimate the power of the press. A tract can stick with a person, go places you can't, and be read at any time by anyone who encounters it. As evangelist Ray Comfort would advise, the only people who don't need Gospel tracts are dead people, Give away those tracts freely.

The Truth Is You Must Simply Go and Proclaim.
SPIRIT-led evangelism requires that you go in faith and proclaim the Gospel of JESUS CHRIST to everyone who will listen. You can't grow in faith unless you go in faith. Arise and go!

Failure to Evangelize Is Betrayal of JESUS.
Peter's greatest sin wasn't murder or adultery but the failure to speak up for JESUS. Fear of speaking up for JESUS is so bad that, according to **Revelation 21:8**, it can land a person in the Lake of Fire:

But for the cowardly, and unbelieving, and abominable, and murderers, and sexually immoral persons, and sorcerers, and idolaters, and all liars, their part *will be* in the lake that burns with fire and brimstone, which is the second death."

Notice that the *cowardly* are listed first, even before the *unbelieving*. It's worse to profess belief in JESUS and shy away from speaking about HIM than it is to not believe in HIM at all. There's a reason the command to not fear appears 365 in the Bible. Each and every day of the year, we are to remind ourselves that fear is not from GOD, and we are to forsake our fears—to crucify our flesh—and speak up for JESUS.

Chances are, you have been cowardly. Don't worry, as worrying can't add a single hour to your life, but do repent—immediately. Ask GOD to forgive you for all the times you denied JESUS by remaining silent instead of speaking up on HIS behalf. If we confess our sins, HE is faithful and just to forgive and cleanse us (**1 John 1:9**). Admitting that silence about JESUS is a sin is the first step to receiving GOD's forgiveness and restoration in this area of our lives. Failure to confess our sin of indifference toward the perishing world around us, or any other sin, results in mental anguish and the wasting away of our bodies. But confessing this sin of betrayal by silence, and any other sins, leads to the comfort, protection, and counsel of GOD in our lives (**Psalm 32**).

Now, get over the guilt of having wasted most of your Christian walk in disobedience to GOD's calling and go confess JESUS to everyone. Trust me, life is so much better when you submit to GOD's will. I had to repent of having wasted almost my entire life operating within carnal ministry models. I haven't been happier since. Trials come, yes, but it's so much easier to see GOD's hand at work in the trials when you finally reach out and grab hold of it, rather than continually batting it away as you grope around trying to do HIS work the world's way.

-4-
Put on the Full Armor of GOD.

Ephesians 6 is not just for Sunday school children. It's a serious call to all saints to armor up for the serious battle in which we're engaged. With constant attacks from our own flesh, the world, and Satan, we cannot survive without GOD's supernatural armor. Suiting up properly is a matter of spiritual life and death for all Christians. Please take a moment to read over this passage of scripture. Then, we will examine each piece of this holy armor.

> **Ephesians 6:14-17**
> [14] Stand firm therefore, HAVING GIRDED YOUR LOINS WITH TRUTH, and HAVING PUT ON THE BREASTPLATE OF RIGHTEOUSNESS, [15] and having shod YOUR FEET WITH THE PREPARATION OF THE GOSPEL OF PEACE; [16] in addition to all, taking up the shield of faith with which you will be able to extinguish all the flaming arrows of the evil *one*. [17] And take THE HELMET OF SALVATION, and the sword of the Spirit, which is the word of God.

Belt of Truth
The belt holds all the armor pieces together. Without it, everything comes undone, and we are naked and exposed, our are loins ungirded, and we are tripping over our unruly clothing, embarrassed and ashamed. The belt of truth is different from the sword of truth, in that the belt is a defensive item of armor, not offensive like the sword. The belt of truth is made up of the truths you know and carry around within you. Without the belt of truth, you will not be able to discern lies from truth, and you are vulnerable to believing that the Satanic accusations made against you are true. If you believe the lies of demons, your belt snaps and you will feel the way you would if your pants literally fell down in public—ashamed.

Remember, it's Satan's goal to shame you and make you feel like a criminal for evangelizing. The truth is that Gospel proclamation is the most loving and meaningful work a person can do with his life. You must keep this truth buckled about your loins at all times if you want to keep covered up and feeling secure while proclaiming the Gospel. To keep your belt strong, read the Bible daily, committing to studying 1-3 chapters each day. We are sanctified by the truth, and the only truth we have is GOD'S word (**John 17:17**). If JESUS upholds the entire universe by the word of HIS power, then we need the truth of GOD's word to uphold the belt of our armor (**Hebrews 1:3**).

As you evangelize with a strong belt, you will be able to take every thought captive, and you will be less likely to entertain Satan's lies about how you're not equipped, qualified, or authorized for the job. Your belt of truth will grow stronger as you continue to evangelize. You will learn truths about sin patterns within all human flesh and how exactly Satan works to sabotage any and all evangelism. You will also learn truths about the laws and principalities that govern certain locations.

I have already listed out many truths for you in this book, but you will discover plenty more for yourself as you obey the LORD's Great Commission. You might even want to keep a running list of the truths GOD teaches you as you go and do HIS work.

Breastplate of Righteousness
The breastplate protects vital organs. Notice it is made of righteousness. Sin is the exact opposite of righteousness. Therefore, sin weakens the breastplate and leaves you open to fatal wounds from the world, Satan, and your own flesh. Be holy as GOD is holy. Otherwise, you will be wounded and ineffective for Kingdom work.

If you continue in unholiness long enough, you will lose your breastplate and be unable to proclaim the Gospel. If you're truly a child of GOD, you can't lose your salvation, but GOD will chastise you in love. HE might even do that through physical suffering or life trials that leave you ineffective for Gospel proclamation for a season. Not all suffering is chastisement from GOD, but the kind that is will keep you sidelined from Gospel work until you confess and flee from your sins (**James 5:16**).

When you depart from righteousness, you damage or lose your breastplate, resulting in an ineffective life for JESUS, thus robbing yourself of eternal rewards. At the end of this Age, when our works stand the fiery test before the throne of GOD, they will burn up and you will be without a crown for all of eternity (**1 Corinthians 3:15**). Let no man take your crown, including your own flesh-man (**Revelation 3:11**). Crucify the flesh daily (**Galatians 5:24**). Seek to bear fruits of the SPIRIT, not thistles of the flesh.

Feet Prepared With the Gospel

You must be ready to explain the Gospel to anyone, anywhere. That's why this book exists, to encourage you to do just that. If you see an opportunity to share the Gospel with someone, even if that opportunity might be brief, seize it. Don't wait for opportunities to happen to you. Keep on the lookout for opportunities. Create them. When out in public, never stop to ask yourself, or anyone else, "Should I talk to that person about JESUS?" If you feel any nudging at all to speak to someone. Say, "Yes LORD," and go immediately to that person with the Gospel.

If you have a successful Gospel conversation, don't congratulate yourself. The Gospel is what saves people. You're just the vessel for the Gospel (**Galatians 2:20, 2 Timothy 2:20-21**). Rejoice in GOD's power, not in your own efforts. On the other hand, if you have a bad interaction, don't stem on it. Any kind of self-congratulation or self-loathing distracts you from the present situation and puts you at risk for losing the next opportunity GOD has for you. Ruminating on your successes and failures is like walking around with your Gospel shoe laces untied. Eventually, you will trip and, perhaps, fall.

I also recommend keeping your feet ready by having Gospel tracts and Bibles ready to distribute at all times. I always carry tracts and Gospels of John in my purse. One of the reason why I like to make my tracts in the form of business cards is that they easily fit into wallets and pockets. I like to keep an open bag of business-card tracts in my pocket whenever I enter a store, and I hand them out like hotcakes as I shop around. If I didn't have my bag of tracts open and ready to go at all times, I would not be able to do this.

Personal Note: Wearing bold JESUS t-shirts is also an effective way to get Gospel conversations started. Most commonly, a bold t-shirt attracts the attention of ministry leaders and other professing Christians, and those conversations usually lead to encouragement and spurring one another on in ministry. Don't be surprised, however, if some of those ministry leaders discourage you, criticize your theology, or distract you from sharing the Gospel with people who actually need to hear it. When a person asks me about my hat or shirt, I usually ask, "Are you an elder or a pastor?" The answer is almost always "yes." I will continue to feel out the person's motives for the conversation from there.

Shield of Faith
While largely defensive, a shield can be used offensively for enemies who dare to come close. The shield can push, slam, create a boundary, and a large shield can even crush toes. Primarily, however, the shield of faith is used to extinguish the fiery arrows of an enemy who stands at a distance because he knows HE's no match for the HOLY SPIRIT who lives inside of you. You guessed it, that enemy is Satan.

If You Lower or Drop Your Shield
Just as Satan got Adam and Eve to let down their guard, their shield so to speak, and to doubt GOD's goodness in the garden, Satan constantly tries to get you to drop your shield of faith. When we face trials in life, we are tempted to doubt GOD's goodness. *Does GOD really have a plan for me? Does HE really work all things together for the good of those who love in HIM? GOD always seems to be blessing other people, but HE seems to want me to struggle.* If we fail to cast out our doubts about GOD's goodness and purpose, we will begin to lower our shield. This is exactly what Satan wants. It's his chance to bombard us with fiery darts.

If you lower your shield for long enough, many fiery darts will strike, and your whole body of armor will be consumed. You will be exposed and easily struck down by any and all spiritual conflicts. You might try to compensate for your lost shield by dodging enemy arrows, but Satan will work tirelessly to harass you with his craftiest archers. As you evangelize, you will start to feel like a criminal for telling people how they can escape Hell and receive the free gift of eternal life in CHRIST. You'll start believing lies, such as Gospel proclamation is a waste of time, or GOD's simple but Great Commission is ineffective in saving souls, or the cross is too offensive to explain to others. Satan will literally burn you out until you forfeit the fight and abandon GOD's simple "go and tell" model for Gospel proclamation.

With charred armor, no shield, and singed skin, you will eventually stop evangelizing and become despondent, even bitter, toward the very idea of evangelizing. You will turn to worldly ministry models that forsake the plain commands JESUS has given to us in the Great Commission. Instead of serving the Gospel, you will serve "sophisticated," and downright Satanic, models of ministry that complicate and subdue Biblical Gospel proclamation. Eventually, Satan might even convince you to pervert the Gospel message by omitting or weakening the topic of Hell, or worse still, persuading you to preach a false "Jesus" who condones the mixing of Christianity with false beliefs or a "Jesus" who excuses the practice of certain sins.

You might even start to resent street preachers and street evangelists and adopt an accusatory mindset toward such, wrongfully thinking that these bold ministers give Christians a bad name. Yes, there are some street ministers with have erroneous theology, but don't let a few poor examples burn your entire outlook on evangelism or mislead you into hatefulness toward your own brothers and sisters in CHRIST.

Hold up that shield of faith and keep those Hellish darts from coming anywhere near you. Remember that JESUS is with us always, that HE always wins, and that GOD really does have a good plan for you. There's a reason why JESUS ends the Great Commission with words that assure us of HIS enduring presence with us (**Matthew 28:20**). And by all means, pray for street ministers. They're doing the work of GOD in ways that most people never will. They are in constant need of HIS empowerment and protection.

At the end of this chapter, I will specifically identify several of Satan's fiery darts so you can be on the defense against them.

The Collective Shield of Faith
We tend to think of the armor of GOD as dresswear for individuals. The shield, however, can also serve as a collective defense system for a group of believers. In ancient times, 27 Roman soldiers could create a turtle

shell, or *testudo* formation, with their shields. Tucked away inside of this formation, the soldiers could advance toward enemy lines without getting struck. What a metaphor! Christians, we must to strive for unity in the faith! If enough of us are unified in true Gospel-faith, imagine the advances we can make against Satan's kingdom. **Be informed:** Unity in worldlines or teachings that contradict the Bible is treason against GOD.

Helmet of Salvation

The first thing Satan attacks for any Christian is the assurance of his or her salvation. He will cause other people, even other Christians, to question your salvation. Some people might flat out tell you you're going to Hell. Others will accuse you of having a critical spirit because you proclaim that JESUS is the only way to Heaven. Other accusers might tell you things like you're unsaved because you don't speak in tongues or fail to manifest some gift of the SPIRIT, or that you've committed some unforgivable sin. **Note:** The only unforgivable sin is blaspheming the HOLY SPIRIT by rejecting the blood of JESUS as the only means for the forgiveness of your sins.

Personal Note: In a great act of mercy and grace, God gave me the gift of tongues late in life, after I'd repented for having doubted the gift for most of my Christian walk. The HOLY SPIRIT testifies to me that the gifts of the SPIRIT are indisputably alive and in operation today. Miracles accompany the believer (**Mark 16:17-18**), but a Christian is not unsaved if he doesn't manifest all the gifts of the SPIRIT or if he is lacking in a particular gift.

Returning to the topic of salvation, why does Satan work so hard to get you to doubt you're saved? Because he knows that if he can make you doubt your salvation, he can break through your helmet and mess up your whole mind, thereby, confusing and damaging your whole being.

If your helmet fails, your head is vulnerable to all kinds of injuries, and if your head is injured, you will be utterly lost and confused. Your mind will be a swamp of unintelligible thoughts. A strike to the head is a blow to your mainframe. This kind of systemic damage to the mind and, thereby to the soul, causes everything else in our lives to become confused and muddled. This is what the enemy wants. Don't give Satan what he wants.

Sometimes, Satan doesn't need to make us doubt our salvation at all. Sometimes, doubts about our salvation arise from our own fleshly fears. If enough doubts arise, we might remove our own helmet. What a tragedy. That being said, doubts about your salvation will definitely come from the outside as well. Don't be caught off guard when colleagues, fellow Christians, family members, friends, and the very people with whom you're trying to share the Gospel question the authenticity of your faith.

Hold fast to your helmet of salvation and be assured that GOD never takes back HIS free gift of eternal life. Remind yourself that nothing can separate us from GOD (**Romans 8:38-39**). We're are in the double grip of the FATHER and the SON (**John 10:27-30**). Even when we are faithless, GOD is faithful (**2 Timothy 2:13**).

When describing salvation to us, there's a reason why JESUS tells us we must be born again of the SPIRIT (**John 3:3**). Think about it, once a baby comes out of the womb, it can't go back inside. The baby can suffer death at any point after birth, but the baby can never be un-birthed. The same principle applies to our rebirth in JESUS. Once we are reborn into the family of GOD, we can't be un-reborn. GOD will never disown a single one of HIS children. HE will never leave us as orphans—even if we behave badly. HE will definitely chastise us, as any good father would, and HE might even take us home early (**1 Corinthians 5:5**). But JESUS will never deny HIMSELF by taking away our salvation (**2 Timothy 2:13**).

Moreover, we're sealed by the HOLY SPIRIT for the day of our redemption (**Ephesians 4:30**). We can't be unsealed by the HOLY SPIRIT. The HOLY SPIRIT is GOD, and if something were to unseal our salvation, that thing would have to be greater than GOD. Ain't gonna happen!

Although I hold firmly to the position that true salvation can't be lost, I don't love the phrase "once saved always saved" because people can be self-deceived about having been saved in the first place. The heart is deceptive above all else (**Jeremiah 17:9**), and the Bible gives us several examples of false teachers and false disciples of Christ. These false converts carry out Kingdom work and even do miracles in JESUS' name, but they are not actually saved (**Matthew 7:21-23**). Judas is arguably the most obvious example of a false convert. He was one of twelve of JESUS' closest disciples. He proclaimed the Kingdom and did signs and wonders in the name of JESUS (**Luke 9:1-2**), yet his name was not written in the Book of Life. JESUS even identified him as a devil (**John 6:70-71**).

The Gospel is so powerful that people can get saved even if an unsaved person proclaims it to them. Likewise, the name of JESUS is so powerful that an unsaved person can speak it, and others can be healed and cleansed of demons. Judas proclaimed the Kingdom and worked wonders in JESUS' name, but he was never saved. Unbelievers today, like Judas, are also able to work miracles and do lying signs and wonders (the story of Balaam in **Numbers 22-24, 2 Thessalonians 2:9-12**).

At the judgment, JESUS will reject many of these professing "Christians" who performed miracles and prophesied in HIS name (**Matthew 7:21-23**). This is why GOD tells us to work out our salvation with fear and trembling (**Philippians 2:12**). Make sure you have believed with all your heart and have been reborn and baptized and sealed by the HOLY SPIRIT.

A good indication that your salvation is true is that you can't practice sin (**1 John 3:6**), and if you try to make a practice of sin, the HOLY SPIRIT convicts you strongly (**John 16:8-11**). If the conviction of the SPIRIT doesn't stop you from practicing sin, then GOD will chastise you (**Hebrews 12:6**). HE will even take you home to be with HIM if you're sinning that badly, but GOD will never take away HIS free gift of salvation from you (**1 Corinthians 5:5**).

If, however, you are practicing sin—that is, you are willfully incorporating a certain sin into your lifestyle, and GOD isn't chastising you—then you might not be saved. It's one thing to be struggling with a sin and desiring to be rid of it. It's another to be content with your sin, justifying it to yourself and others, and accepting it as part of who you are and not trying to change anything about that. If you are practicing sin and thinking GOD is okay with it, then you are worshipping a false "God," an idol of your imagination. You have accepted another "gospel."

You believe in a false "Jesus," and you have received a false "Holy Spirit" **(2 Corinthians 11 and 1 John 3 and 4)**. Repent immediately and believe in the true JESUS. The true JESUS died to free you from sin. He didn't die so you could make mockery of HIS blood by condoning, enabling, partaking in, and celebrating sinful lifestyles.

Sword of the Spirit

The sword is the primary offensive piece of the armor of GOD. The sword of the SPIRIT is supernatural, and it is the only weapon that can drive away Satan's workers of iniquity and save a soul from Hell. This sword is shaper than any two-edged sword man can forge because it is not manmade. And it's certainly not made of metal but, rather, of the very word of GOD, which is so sharp that it divides soul and spirit **(Hebrews 4:12)**. When you speak the Gospel, recite a verse of scripture, or give out Gospel tracts, you are wielding this supernatural sword.

Actually, it's the HOLY SPIRIT HIMSELF who wields the sword through you. The sword of the SPIRIT belongs to the HOLY SPIRIT. While the HOLY SPIRIT wields the sword, HE will never override our personal will or intellect, but HE will use our intellect to fight spiritual battles through us. The SPIRIT teaches us all things and calls to remembrance the words of the Bible as we need them in conversation. How useful we are to the SPIRIT depends on how much of ourselves we have submitted to GOD's will and word. Have we sought GOD with all our heart? Have we admitted to and repented from specific sins? Have we crucified our flesh? Have we torn down all idols in our lives? Have we trusted in GOD alone to meet our needs? OR are we trusting in others? Are we depending on our own strength, education, money, charm, and skills? Most importantly, have we faithfully studied the word?

The more scripture you know, the sharper your sword, and the more scripture the SPIRIT has available to bring to your remembrance as you engage in Gospel conversations. I cannot express to you the importance of not just reading, but memorizing scripture. You will be amazed at how easily foes are toppled by the word of GOD, which is living and active and pierces to the division of soul and of spirit **(Hebrews 4:12)**.

Any false religion, cult, or false belief can be slain by just a handful of Bible verses. I especially like to have easy access to the verses that prove JESUS is CO-CREATOR with the FATHER, the SON OF GOD, that HE is ONE with the FATHER, and supreme over all things—visible and invisible, including Satan and the angels (**Colossians 1:15-19**). Yes, JESUS even created Satan, who was once beautiful but fell from grace when he rebelled against GOD (**Isaiah 14, Ezekiel 28**). Satan especially hates the reality that he's a created being. HE's viciously jealous of JESUS—the uncreated, eternal SON OF GOD.

Bare Essential Verses for Gospel Battle

Please memorize a few key verses for use in the heat of battle, that is, during evangelistic conversations. Start by remembering the number 1. Then, memorize these key verses, which are all located in the first chapter of their corresponding books of the Bible. These verses prove JESUS is GOD IN FLESH, that all things were created through HIM, and that JESUS and the FATHER ARE ONE.

- **Genesis 1:1-3 & John 1:1-3 (Bonus: John 10:30.** It's short!)
- **Colossians 1:15-17**
- **Hebrews 1:1-3**

When you've got these verses memorized, I recommend adding the verses surrounding them to your memory bank as well. You will also want to add key verses about salvation to your repertoire, such as the following:

- **John 1:12-13**
- **John 3:3**
- **John 3:16-18**
- **John 14:6**
- **Romans 6:23**
- **1 Corinthians 15:3-4**
- **Ephesians 2:8-9**

Challenge yourself, and try to memorize an entire Psalm or chapter of scripture this year. The more scripture you have memorized, the more maneuvers of the sword the HOLY SPIRIT has to work with as HE guides you in spiritual warfare.

You will use many other Bible passages in addition to the ones I've listed here when evangelizing. The ones I've listed are not even a fraction of what you will find yourself referencing as you engage in Gospel conversations. I suggest writing down the verses you find yourself referencing most frequently and memorizing those. You don't have to know the exact chapter and verse reference when you start evangelizing. Precision will come as GOD sharpens your sword through battles.

Don't let your lack of Bible knowledge keep you from going with the Gospel. It's okay for now if you don't have anything memorized. Just get going with the Gospel. The memorization and equipping will come. Seek first GOD's kingdom, HE will supply all you need along the way (**Matthew 6:33**).

What Are the Fiery Darts From Satan?

Simply put, Satan's fiery darts are any accusations and excuses people give to justify their rejection of JESUS and make you feel guilty for trying to share the Gospel with them. Notice that Satan cowardly crouches on the rooftop, far from battle lines, and shoots arrows from a distance. We must still be vigilant against these darts. Satan has the higher ground, and his accusations can destroy us if we let down our shield. I have already identified several ways Satan will use people to oppose you before you start evangelizing. And he will definitely send out his workers of iniquity to oppose you while you evangelize.

Don't be surprised if such people stoop so low as to attack you personally, mocking your appearances, criticizing how your children are dressed, how you're a bad parent for not "educating" your child about poisonous false beliefs, complaining about how you've failed to give them something other than the Gospel, scolding you for not having your husband with you, making inappropriate lustful remarks, giving you advice about how you should try more subtle, intelligent, or trendy ways of reaching people for JESUS...

In addition to making accusations against you, many people will give all kinds of excuses for not accepting JESUS. The list below identifies some of these common excuses. These excuses are actually veiled accusations against Christians, churches, and GOD HIMSELF.

Satan will often conceal his fiery darts as sob stories, deceiving his actors into playing the role of a "victim" who has been damaged beyond repair by a church or a Christian. Sadly, bad church experiences are a reality, but JESUS is greater than any pain we have ever experienced, and HE commands us to forgive everyone. Even the worst of church experiences does not entitle a person to reject JESUS and withhold forgiveness toward others. Everyone will stand in judgment before GOD, perpetrators and victims alike. You can't control whether or not the person who harmed you will ever ask for forgiveness, but you can control your own willingness to forgive.

GOD will not take excuses on Judgment Day—not a single one. No lying statement on the list below, nor any other excuse you hear, is going to persuade GOD to overlook the fact that a person has rejected the precious blood of HIS SON. Brothers and sisters, please be sure the people you speak with understand that. GOD has a zero tolerance policy for the rejection of JESUS.

Personal Note: When I encounter people who plead "church hurt," I sometimes say something like, "I'm sorry you have been so mistreated in the church, but has JESUS ever done you wrong?" Most people will say "no." Some people might accuse JESUS of not being present during their abuse. To that I reply, "He must have answered your prayers at some point because you're standing here today, free from your abusers." If the person is still suffering abuse, which is rarely the case, you may have to bring the information to the proper authorities. Please do your research and be wise.

Bottom line is this: Each human gets one lifetime to decide one way or the other about JESUS (**Hebrews 9:27-28**). If the person with whom you're speaking doesn't want to forgive others and accept JESUS, then at least you did your part in attempting to share the Gospel.

Excuses That Won't Work on Judgment Day

The list below spells out some of the most common excuses, or fiery darts, a person in unbelief will shoot at you during a conversation. To make things more interesting, I have written these excuses from the perspective of a person standing before JESUS on Judgment Day.

- Sorry, JESUS, I didn't think we'd meet so soon. I was going to commit to YOU at some point.
- I thought I would have time to clean myself up before I had to answer to YOU.
- JESUS, I thought you were just a man. I had no idea YOU are GOD IN THE FLESH and that YOU were going to judge me.
- I couldn't find in the Bible where YOU said YOU were GOD.
- I couldn't understand the TRINITY and gave up on Christianity.
- I didn't think judging people was YOUR style.
- I didn't think Hell was real, and I didn't realize I needed YOU to save me from it.
- I thought teaching people about Hell was a threatening and manipulative way to force GOD on them.
- I thought YOU would accept me just as I am.
- I thought YOU were forgiving and would pardon everyone. I didn't realize I had to believe in the cross.
- I didn't realize there was only one way to Heaven and that YOU are IT.
- I thought all religions were basically the same and that YOU would accept anyone who believed in a higher power.
- I just couldn't believe someone as powerful as YOU died on a cross.
- I thought YOUR resurrection was symbolic, or spiritual, or something people made up.
- I had bad experiences at church and gave up on YOU.
- I was raised in a false religion. I didn't know any better.
- Hypocritical Christians made me forsake YOU.
- I felt judged at church.
- I thought church was for women, children, and weak people who needed help.
- I was taught people made up the existence of GOD to improve their chances of survival. I didn't realize GOD was real.
- The Crusades made me think Christianity was evil.
- I thought street preachers were a bad representation of how Christians should behave, so I just stayed away from religion.
- I thought YOU were all about love and would never tell people they have to repent.
- I didn't think anyone could know for sure how to get to Heaven.

- Religion is such a complicated and a loaded topic. I thought avoiding it was the best way to live a peaceful life and love others.
- I thought the whole religion thing was a scam to make money.
- I thought it was selfish of people to want to live in paradise in the next life. We should be content with the life we have.
- No one ever invited me to church.
- My friend was kicked out of a church for a lifestyle choice and that left a bad taste in my mouth.
- I didn't realize I was living in unrepentant sin.
- The Bible was too fantastical for me to believe.
- My parents were too pushy with church.
- My parents sent me to public school. I didn't stand a chance against the culture around me.
- Everyone in my field of study was an atheist, and we all believed in evolution. What else was I supposed to do?
- I had no choice but to live in unrepentant sin because YOU gave me bad parents.
- My life was too hard. It's YOUR fault for not making it easier for me to believe in YOU.
- I thought it was arrogant of YOU to want me to bow down and worship YOU.
- How could I have lived my life to the fullest if I was busy worshipping YOU all the time?
- I lived a good life. I was a good person. I raised a family, was faithful to my job, gave to charity, got baptized, played piano at church...
- I went to confession, took communion, and prayed to Mary and all the saints.
- I tried my best to follow the Ten Commandments.
- My pastor told me I was saved. I thought I was good to go.
- My Daddy was a pastor.
- If YOU wanted me to enter Heaven, why didn't YOU force me to believe in YOU?
- YOU are the one who made me gay.
- I couldn't believe in YOU because there's too much evil in the world.

-5-
Prepare Your Materials For Evangelism

If the thought of making preparations and reading checklists doesn't excite you, and you just want to jump into evangelizing, then feel free to skip this chapter and begin the 21 evangelism tasks, referring back to this chapter as needed. You might want to at least skim over the lists in this chapter to see the kinds of items you will need. Remember, you don't need any items at all to begin evangelizing. Feel free to rip off the Band-Aid and head out your door with the Gospel—without reading another word in this book. Praise GOD if you do!!!

If you're running an evangelism course or plan to lead others in the competition of these 21 tasks, then you will probably want to read this chapter. You can collect your evangelism materials ahead of time or acquire them as you go through the 21 tasks. If you're planning to do all 21 tasks in 21 consecutive days, then I recommend gathering most, if not all, the materials listed here ahead of time.

If you will be completing these 21 tasks with a group, then I highly recommend the group leaders read through this list and look at the assignments ahead of time to determine what to buy or assign to group members to acquire. Group leaders can tell group members what to purchase week-by-week or send them home with a checklist for supplies.

Materials Needed for Personal Bible Study and Prayer
___A Bible for your personal reading time. Please use whatever translation you prefer. **Personal Note:** My favorite translations are KJV, NKJV, NASB (1995), and ESV. I prefer literal translations over interpretations, and I try to avoid translations that take lots of liberties, resorting to those only if no other option is available.

___Earplugs or noise cancelling headphones to limit distractions while reading the Bible and praying. Do not play any music or media while reading and praying, and please only use white noise if you must.
___Appropriate groceries if you will be fasting.
___Notebook, pencils, pens, highlighters, and any other school supplies you like to use during your personal Bible study time.
___For focused prayer time, please gather any lists that will help you, such as a church directory or list of birthdays for the month in your church or Christian group. I also recommend you take down names or get a copy of the rosters from the groups or classes you're involved in so you have specific names to pray over. It's true that JESUS knows everyone's names, but I find it meaningful and helpful to pray over people by name whenever possible. **Personal Note:** I suggest recording names to pray over in columns in a notebook and praying over 1-2 columns of names each day. A standard notebook or composition book will easily fit two columns of names on each page.
___A prayer calendar, list of countries, or list of prayer requests for persecuted Christians around the world. Organizations like *Voice of the Martyrs* supply prayer calendars. You should be able to request a calendar from their website at *persecution.com*. Use such lists during prayer time. See the *EVANGELIZE GEORGIA* website if you would like free video guides and handouts about on how to pray and fast: https://evangelizegeorgia.org/free-guide-to-fasting/
___A list of world and national news items to pray over for focused prayer time. Make sure to research Israel in particular, as GOD commands us to pray for the peace of Jerusalem (**Psalm 122:6**).

Main Materials Needed for the 21 Evangelism Assignments
___A notecard for sending to a friend (not needed if you send an email or text instead)
___JESUS t-shirt if you don't have one, or the supplies to make one, such as a t-shirt, stencils, and fabric paint.. The assignment for Day 3 is to order, make, or buy a JESUS shirt. You can wait until then to order your shirt, or you can get ahead of the game and order it now. Please do not wear shirts that mock or joke about JESUS or shirts that add something to JESUS, such as "JESUS Plus Coffee Is All I Need." JESUS plus nothing is all anyone needs. You can find JESUS t-shirts on *Amazon*, or you can support various ministries by purchasing shirts

through them, such as this site from street minister **Nicholas Bowling**: https://store.nicholasbowling.com/
___Clipboard or notebook for writing down prayer requests and the names of the people with whom you speak.
___A JESUS yard sign or the supplies to make one. **Optional:** A door poster, car magnet, or bumper sticker. The assignment on Day 5 is to order or make a yard sign. You can get a JESUS sign that's appropriate for an upcoming holiday or one that works for any time of year. If you live in an apartment or a dorm, consider hanging a JESUS sign or poster on your door, or opt for a car magnet or bumper sticker instead. If you're willing and able, buy all of the JESUS things and make your whole life one giant billboard for JESUS. If you will be making your own sign, you will need items like poster board, stakes, sharpies, markers, paint, stencils, a ruler, stickers...
___At least 4 cheap giveaway Bibles. New Testaments or The Gospel of John are fine for giveaways. The Dollar Tree usually carries New Testaments. They sometimes have mini KJV New Testaments, though the text is small. Otherwise, the translations they sell may not be great. That's okay for this assignment. No credible English translation of the Bible has ever gotten the death, burial, and resurrection of Christ wrong—unless it's a corrupt translation from a false religion or cult. You can also order Gospels of John from sites like *Amazon*. They usually sell them individually or in bundles of 10 or 25. Consider buying a few Gospels of John or Bibles in Spanish as well. Goodwill is also an option for finding cheap Bibles. **Personal Note:** I like to buy Gospels of John in bulk from sites like *biblesinbulk.com*, but you need not do that unless you're going to commit to giving away 200+ Bibles in the near future...which would be a great long-term goal to have!
___A small gift you would like to bring to a neighbor. I usually bring a package of store-bought cookies.
___At least 10 Gospel Tracts. You can print free tracts from the *EVANGELIZE GEORGIA* website. Link and QR code given at the start of this book. You can also use your own tract, which you will be making on Days 8-10 and 13. Or you can order Gospel tracts from **Ray Comfort's** *Living Waters* website:
https://livingwaters.com/product-category/gospel-tracts/
Be careful to get tracts that clearly state the Gospel of JESUS CHRIST and are honest about Hell being a place of eternal torment, not just a place of separation from God. **Personal Note:** I recommend having well

over 10 Gospel tracts on hand for use during and after this program is through. I like to have a few thousand tracts in stock at all times. After completing these 21 days, it's my prayer that you will see every holiday and occasion you can think of as a reason to hand out Gospel tracts.

___A FREEE PRAYER sign, which you can print from the *EVANGELIZE GEORGIA* website (given at the start of this book).

___A printer. Please make sure you have the means to print your own Gospel tracts and a FREE PRAYER sign. If you will be using your own printer, make sure you have ink and paper. You can use plain computer paper for all the evangelism assignments in this book. For best results, I suggest using colorful paper or cardstock, especially for the sign.

___A laminate sheet, clear folder, page protector, or cellophane and tape to protect the FREE PRAYER sign you will be printing.

Gospel Goodie Bag Supplies (Optional for Day 18, but Highly Recommended)
Please buy enough goodie bag supplies to make at least 5 Gospel goodie bags. You can always use the extra supplies to continue with evangelism after completing your 21 tasks. What makes this Gospel goodie bag a *Gospel* goodie bag is that fact that you will be including a Gospel tract in addition to your choice of goodies. Here is a suggested checklist of items for each bag:
- Clear sandwich bags or Ziplocs for holding all the items
- A 1.5-inch sticker to seal or decorate the bag
- Gospel tract
- Candy or small non-candy prizes like stickers or wristbands (optional but recommended)
- Church business cards or brochures or flyers to upcoming local Christian events
- School supplies or earplugs (optional, good for college students)
- Small stress relief items, such as rubber bands (optional)
- Mini Bible or Gospel of John (optional, but recommended)
- Doorhanger Bags (optional). A doorhanger is exactly what it sounds like, a clear plastic bag that can be hung from a doorknob. You can put out doorhangers in addition to, or instead of, handing out Gospel goodie bags. If you don't want to order doorhanger bags online, you can always use string to turn your Gospel goodie bag into a doorhanger.

Personal Note: I keep my Gospel goodie bags super simple because I go through a lot of them quickly. I use sandwich bags, and I include a church brochure, a business-card tract, QR code to a free online Bible, QR codes to Bible comics and movies, and a piece of hard candy or gum. I can easily adapt my goodie bags into doorhangers by adding a few items. My doorhangers are geared toward families and include small seasonal prizes and items like children's Bible stories, QR codes to kids Bible shows/movies, coloring pages, and stickers.

Blessing Bag Supplies
Think of a blessing bag as an expanded Gospel goodie bag with helpful items for emergency living situations. Here are the supplies you will need for each blessing bag:
- Quart-sized Ziploc bag
- Gospel tract and QR codes to an online Bible and Christian media
- Church brochure or business card
- 8-ounce bottle of water
- Washcloth
- Mini pack of tissues
- A few band aids
- A toothbrush
- Mini toothpaste
- Floss or floss toothpicks
- Chewing gum
- Mints
- Snacks (optional). Some people also like to put granola bars and crackers in their blessing bags.

Food Gift Card Alternative (Optional)
If you don't have the time to make a blessing bag, consider buying a gift card for a meal. For an extra bonus, you could include a gift card in your blessing bag. I suggest a 10.00 card to a fast food restaurant that anyone can access anywhere, such as McDonald's. If you buy grocery store gift cards, please make sure items like alcohol and cigarettes can't be purchased using the cards.

Personal Note: I like to have meal gift cards on me all times in case people ask me for money while I'm evangelizing. Instead giving of cash, I prefer to give them something they can use for food. Sure, the gift card can be traded for a bad substance, but at least I did my part to not send the person away empty handed. DO NOT GIVE OUT MONEY and carefully vet every situation so you may present yourself before the throne of JESUS as good steward of HIS resources. True, a person can barter with almost any item you give him, but we must do our part to meet needs. Giving away "basic need items" in lieu of cash allows us to do that with less risk of fueling an addiction.

Large Blessing Bag (Optional)
You may also use gallon bags for your blessing bags and fill them generously with all kinds of items in addition to the ones listed here. Quart-sized bags are generally easier to handle, but please do as the HOLY SPIRIT leads you. If using a gallon bag, consider adding these items:
- New Testament Bible or Gospel of John
- Roll of toilet paper
- Deodorant
- Soap
- Hand Sanitizer
- Socks
- T-shirt (L or XL)
- Package of wipes
- Small flashlight
- Magnifying bookmark if Bible is small print

Personal Note: I stay away from snack items unless I know I'll be handing out the bags right away. Otherwise, the snacks don't do well in my car, especially in summer heat.

Snack Pack Supplies (An Alternative or Addition to a Blessing Bag)
If you would like to supply snacks to those in need, I suggest you keep those separate from hygiene items, and make a different bag, which I call a "snack pack." A snack pack is a quart-sized bag with just snacks in it. Feel free to fill a gallon bag if you so desire. Keeping snacks separated in their own bag allows you to keep an eye on expiration dates, and the snacks won't absorb any scents from the hygiene items.

For snacks, consider soft foods for those who might have dental issues. And please make sure packages are easy to open and won't require additional tools, such as a can opener or scissors. Here are some suggestions for snack pack items:
- Quart-sized bag for storing items
- Gospel tract and QR codes to an online Bible or Movie
- Church brochure or business card
- 8-ounce bottle of water
- Plastic spoon or fork
- Napkins, tissues, or handwipes
- Jell-O
- Applesauce
- Pudding
- Packaged fruit
- Granola Bars
- Crackers, pretzels, or crackers with filling
- Fruit snacks
- Dried fruit
- Nuts

Bonus Materials for Setting Up a Prayer Tent and Helping Needy Communities.

If you are able to set up a Prayer Tent, which is just what it sounds like—a tent from which you minister the Gospel, pray with people, and help to meet basic needs—you will need supplies for that. You can find checklists for setting up a Prayer Tent and supplies needed for ministering to the needy on the *EVANGELIZE GEORGIA* website. Link and QR code given at the start of this book.

21 EVANGELISM ASSIGNMENTS

DAY 1

Stand for JESUS.

Enter HIS Gates With Thanksgiving.
Thank GOD for letting you live during a time of history in which you have access to many types of media and can post messages about JESUS that can instantly be read by others around the world. Thank HIM for your freedom of speech, which came at a high price to those who gave their lives to establish and preserve it. **Pray** that GOD will give you HIS boldness and wisdom to make it clear to others you're on team JESUS.

The Task
Change your email signature and social media status to show you're on team JESUS. If you have no idea how to do any of this and are terrified of technology, then please skip down to the last two paragraphs of this section.

Otherwise, get creative with your online profiles. Maybe include a short Gospel explanation or favorite verses of scripture in your description. As an example, my profile on my *X* account says, "JESUS is the SON OF GOD. He died on the cross for our sins, and GOD raised HIM to life. Believe and receive eternal life." My tagline on the *EVANGELIZE GEORGIA* website is "JESUS created you. HE died on the cross to recreate you." My email signature includes **John 3:16-18**.

Whatever it is you decide to do with your email signatures and social media profiles, make it as clear to the world as possible that you believe JESUS is GOD IN FLESH, that HE died on the cross for you sins, was buried, and rose on the third day. This task may take longer than 15 minutes if you have several email accounts or are active on multiple social media platforms. **Caution:** Please use your discernment with any work email accounts or professional platforms.

In addition to updating your profiles, please call, text, or email your church and ask to be placed on the prayer list because you will be evangelizing.

Group Suggestion: If your church, home fellowship, or Christian Group has a website or email account, consider updating the tagline or email signature to include a Gospel Bible verse or a simple Gospel statement. To make things fun, you could have everyone in the group submit a suggestion for a Gospel tagline, and then vote on the best one.

DAY 2
Thinking of You

Enter HIS Gates With Thanksgiving.
Thank GOD for the materials you will be using for this assignment. Thank HIM for your hands and your eyes, for the ability to read and write, and for the people who taught you how to do so. Ask GOD for HIS wisdom and words for ministering to a dearly loved unbeliever in your life.

The Task
Write a short note, text, or email to an unbelieving friend or family member telling her you're thinking about and praying for her. Include **John 3:16-18** inside the note or on a separate page. You might also want to include the FREE GIFT Gospel tract, available on the *EVANGELIZE GEORGIA* website. The website and QR code are given at the front of this book.

Bonus Assignment: After completing the 21 evangelism tasks in this book (or sooner if you're ready), follow up with the recipient of your message. A phone call would be best. If you're not sure how to get the conversation going, consider the following talking points.
- Remind the person you've been praying for her.
- Ask about the person's life, family, job…
- Give a brief update about your own life.
- Ask if the person would like prayer for anything specific.
- Ask to pray with the person over the phone, and pray.
- Ask if the person has given anymore thought to JESUS.
- Whenever possible, present the Gospel of JESUS CHRIST (**1 Corinthians 15:1-4**) or read a few Gospel Bible verses to the

person, such as the Romans Road or **John 3:16-18**. If you don't know what the Romans Road is, then your **other bonus assignment** is to look it up and to highlight or underline the verses of the Romans Road in your Bible. You might even want to put tabs in your Bible so you can easily locate the verses when explaining the Gospel to others.
- Let the HOLY SPIRIT guide the conversation.

Group Suggestion: Have a "Notecard Night" (or day) for your Christian group. Set up tables with scratch paper, notecards, and pens on them. Have everyone draft a note on scratch paper first, and then share their draft out loud with the group or a partner. After receiving feedback from others, everyone should copy their revised notes onto a nice notecard. **OR** if group members prefer email or text, each person could take his drafted note home and send it in either of those ways.

It might also be neat to have a group leader text his or her messages at the group meeting. If the recipient responds right then and there, the group leader could furthering the dialog, and everyone could be praying as the conversation continues live.

DAY 3

Be a Billboard for JESUS.

Enter HIS Gates With Thanksgiving.
Thank GOD for the money to buy a t-shirt or the supplies you will be purchasing to make one. Thank HIM for the freedom you have to wear personal items that represent JESUS and for the men and women who fought to preserve such freedoms for you. Ask GOD for the wisdom to buy or design just the right t-shirt that will bring the most glory to JESUS.

The Task
Order, buy, or make a JESUS t-shirt. The shirt should clearly and boldly have the name JESUS on it, and it should edify HIM or point people to the cross. Stay away from shirts that make jokes with JESUS' holy name

or mock HIM in any way. Please also stay away from JESUS shirts that add something to JESUS, such as "JESUS Plus Coffee Is All I Need." JESUS plus nothing is all anyone needs. Church shirts are great, but a church shirt doesn't count for this task unless it boldly displays the name of JESUS.

You can find JESUS t-shirts on *Amazon*, or you can support various ministries by purchasing shirts through them, such as this site from street minister, **Nicholas Bowling**: https://store.nicholasbowling.com/

Whenever the t-shirt arrives, wear it in public. Be sure to wear it on days when you go evangelizing. If you already have a JESUS shirt, then get it out and wear it in public this week.

Group Suggestion: Have your group make t-shirts with stencils and fabric paint or iron-on letters. You can order the supplies online or buy them at a craft store or a large department store with a craft section. **OR** have each person make up a JESUS t-shirt logo, and let the group vote on their favorite. The group leader, or someone with design skills, could then design a t-shirt with the winning logo and have shirts printed. For larger groups, consider breaking everyone into teams, and have each team submit a logo for consideration by the whole group.

DAY 4
Prayer Walk...or Drive

Enter HIS Gates With Thanksgiving.
Thank GOD for able legs, your car, bike, wheelchair, or whatever means of transportation HE has given you. Thank HIM for the privilege of interceding for your community in prayer. Thank GOD for the freedom to be able to walk around your neighborhood, and **pray** in JESUS' name. Thank HIM for the men and women who fought to establish and preserve your freedoms.

The Task

Walk or drive through your neighborhood and **pray** for your neighbors. Ask GOD to open doors for sharing the Gospel with them. **Pray** for the protection, salvation, and prosperity of every household. **Pray** over as many people by name as you can. Please exercise caution whenever walking through neighborhoods. Don't go at night, and take a buddy whenever possible.

Bonus Assignment: All week (and beyond), **pray** for opportunities to share the Gospel as you drive through your town, walk through a store or go anywhere I public. As you do this, look for needy communities and neighborhoods. Look for areas where people seem to take breaks and spend leisure time. Write down your observations and ask GOD to guide you in future evangelism to these people and places. Ask GOD to raise up many workers for the fields. **Also,** keep watch for any bulletin boards and tables where you can freely leave Gospel tracts and flyers for Christian events.

Extra Bonus: Have Gospel tracts on you as you go about your prayer walk, and leave some at public tables or on bulletin boards. Maybe even put each tract inside a Ziploc bag, and leave the bags somewhere visible. **Pray** that the person who needs it the most will find it.

Group Suggestion: Do a prayer walk or drive as a group. If the group meets at the church, then consider walking around a nearby neighborhood or the church itself. Make sure everyone has a buddy, and don't go after dark. If it's dark outside during your group meeting time, simply walk around the church building and **pray** over the rooms and the activities that take place there. Always remember to **pray** for workers and employees.

DAY 5

Front-Lawn Evangelism

Enter HIS Gates With Thanksgiving.

Thank GOD for the means to buy or create the sign you will be placing in your front yard. Ask HIM for HIS wisdom to post just the right words that will point people to salvation in JESUS CHRIST.

The Task
Order or make a JESUS yard sign. Put up the sign when it arrives, or put it out for an upcoming holiday. For best results, make sure the sign is weather proof and stake it properly into the ground. At the very least, Keep the sign out until you finish the rest of these evangelism tasks, or keep it up forever, replacing it with fresh signs as needed.

If you make your own sign, get creative. Use bold colors and images to get the message across. You can order a sign online on sites like *Amazon*, or you can custom design your own sign through a print-on-demand website, such as *VistaPrint* or *Printly*. If you decide to design your own sign and have never done so before then, this assignment will probably take 30-45 minutes from start to finish, possibly longer depending on any number of factors. Remember, church signs don't count for this assignment. Evangelism is JESUS promotion, not church advertisement.

If you live in an apartment or a dorm and cannot put out a yard sign, then consider posting a sign on your front door, or opt for a car magnet or bumper sticker for your car.

Bonus: Do all of the above. Put up a yard sign, a door poster, a bumper sticker on the back of your car, and car magnets on the sides of your car. Here are just a few ideas for sign slogans. Have fun and get creative with your own slogans.
- JESUS died for our sins. (Passover/Good Friday/All Year)
- JESUS lives. Believe and live. (Resurrection Sunday / All year)
- JESUS SAVES
- JESUS sets you free.
- JESUS makes you new.
- JESUS: SAVIOR. LORD. GOD IN FLESH.
- JESUS is coming.
- Ready 4 JESUS?
- FREE entry to Heaven. JESUS paid it all.
- GOD sent HIS SON JESUS. Believe. (Christmas)

Group Suggestion: Have a "Sign Night" with your Christian group and let everyone make their own sign. The group leader(s) will need to buy poster materials beforehand, or the week prior, assign group members the task of bringing in supplies. **OR** have each person or smaller groups within the group suggest sign slogans. Write down the slogans and have a panel of judges or the whole group vote on their favorites. The group leader could then have the top 1-3 slogans printed up as signs and make those signs available to group members to take home and post on their lawns.

For added fun, have group members take pictures with their posted signs, and text the pictures to the group leader for posting to the group *Facebook* page or website.

At the following meeting, have everyone share their feelings and experiences. Don't be surprised if some people are embarrassed to have a sign or bumper sticker on their property. Encouraged such group members to not to be ashamed of the Gospel. Cast out the spirit of fear if necessary.

DAY 6

Buy Giveaway Bibles.

Enter HIS Gates With Thanksgiving.
Thank GOD for the money with which to buy Bibles. Thank HIM that you live in a country where Bibles can be freely bought and sold in stores. Thank GOD for the men and women who fought, and still fight, to make that freedom a reality for you.

The Task
Buy at least 4 cheap Bibles to give away. As of the time I'm writing this book, Dollar Tree sells New Testaments. They sometimes carry KJV. Sometimes, they even carry larger New Testaments with nice-sized print. If they don't carry KJV, the available translations may not be great. The translation doesn't matter that much for this assignment. No credible

English translation of the Bible has ever gotten the death, burial, and resurrection of Christ wrong.

Feel free to buy more than 4 Bibles. The more you buy, the more you can give away, and the more opportunities people will have to read GOD's word. If you really want to get into giving away Bibles, then feel free to order them in bulk from biblesinbulk.com or a Christian wholesaler of your choice. I highly recommend you buy a single Bible before making a bulk order, and make sure the print is a good size. I only order Bibles that say "large" or "extra-large" print. If someone donates small print Bibles to our ministry, I hand those out to college students, who usually have good-working eyes. You might also want to include a magnifying bookmark with the smaller print Bibles.

Personal Note: I buy the Gospel of John (ESV or NIV) by the case for handing out on campuses and street and for general witnessing and for placing inside Project Christmas Child shoeboxes. I give away hundreds of Gospels of John every year. They are small, lightweight, and easy to handle.

I don't love the NIV translation because it is too interpretive, but the NIV Gospels of John are generally the cheapest and serve the purpose of getting the Gospel message into people's hands at a budget price.

Bonus: Watch the free Evangelism Crash Course video series on the *EVANGELIZE GEORGIA* website. Link and QR code given at the front of this book. The 4 videos total 87 minutes. If you don't have time to watch the course today, then try to watch it on another day, or watch one video per day over the next few days.

Group Suggestion: Have your church or Christian group take up a collection to buy giveaway Bibles or bulk Gospels of John. You might even want to host a fundraiser, such as a bake sale, car wash, t-shirt sale, Sunday morning coffee bar, holiday market, garage sale, or an event to which you charge admission or charge for snacks. Once the funds are secured, the group leader or someone in the group, could order the Bibles. When the Bibles arrive, give out a determined number of them to each group member. **OR** Have group members run a Bible collection at their home churches. Each member could ask his or her congregation to buy cheap large print Bibles and place them in a box somewhere at the church by a certain date. Group members can then divide the Bibles whichever way the group leader thinks is best.

DAY 7
Bless People With Bibles.

Enter HIS Gates With Thanksgiving.
Thank GOD for able legs, your car, bike, wheelchair, or whatever means of transportation HE has given you. Thank HIM for the opportunity to bless your community with the word of GOD. Ask GOD for HIS wisdom in distributing your gift Bibles. Ask HIM to help you to obey the HOLY SPIRIT, even if that means changing your original plans for GOD's superior plans.

The Task
Give away at least 3 of the Bibles you purchased yesterday. Try putting them in a "My Little Library" in your neighborhood or a nearby neighborhood. **Or** walk around your neighborhood and hand out the Bibles to teenagers (or whomever) you meet.

I have found that most people will take a Bible or tract if you hand it to them while telling them you wanted to bless them with a gift from your church. And, yes, the Bible is a gift from your church, even if you bought it with your own money because you are a part of the church universal. You are the church, so any blessing from you, a member of the church, is a blessing from the church.

Don't be discouraged if someone doesn't want a Bible. **Pray** for that person, especially for his or her salvation if you suspect the person is unsaved. Praise GOD if the person's reason for not wanting a Bible is that HE already has one and would like you to bless someone who needs it.

Be Informed: Don't be surprised if neighbors remove your Bibles from the "Little Libraries." Even some churchgoing professing "Christians" will do this under the Satanic influence of wanting to keep neighborhood items "religiously neutral." There's no such thing as spiritual neutrality, and there's certainly nothing neutral about a "My Little Library" that contains nothing but godless literature that promotes sexual immorality, sorcery, fantasies, and "scientific" books written by authors who deny the undeniable scientific evidence for GOD THE CREATOR (**Romans 18-20**). A person is either with JESUS or against HIM (**Matthew 12:30**).

Bonus Assignment: At Halloween, hand out Bibles or Gospels of John for trick-or-treaters. You can even tape a piece of candy to the cover or make goodie bags with a small Bible inside. Get creative and have fun.

Group Suggestion: Have your Christian group or smaller groups within the group drive or walk around and put Bibles into "My Little Libraries." The group might also make stops and hand out Bibles to people they meet along the way or see along the road. Please do this activity during the day and use best practices for safety.

DAY 8

Brainstorm Your Own Tract.

Enter HIS Gates With Thanksgiving.
Thank GOD for supplying the sample Gospel tracts you'll be studying. Thank HIM for the evangelists who have gone before you in making those tracts. Ask GOD for HIS wisdom in brainstorming a tract that will bring glory to HIM through a clear and effective Gospel presentation.

The Task
Read sample Gospel tracts on the internet at *Living Waters* and any others you can find online or in print. *Living Waters* tracts are available on the website here:
https://livingwaters.com/product-category/gospel-tracts/

Brainstorm how you would create your own tract. You don't ever have to use the tract you will be making on Day 9, but the exercise of creating

one is a fun way to practice presenting the Gospel. As you brainstorm your tract, ask yourself the following questions and ponder the answers:
- What size and format would you make your tract? Brochure, mini brochure, business card, business card tent, greeting card, flyer, postcard?
- How would you communicate to a person that he can be a new creation—free of sin and death—by trusting in the death, burial, and resurrection of JESUS CHRIST?
- How would you express that only as a new creature is a person fit to live in paradise with GOD forever?
- How would you convey that JESUS is GOD IN FLESH, the SON OF GOD, MESSIAH, and that HE is the only way to Heaven?
- How would you explain that the consequence of unbelief is eternal torment in the Lake of Fire?
- What would your tract look like?
- Would you put any images on the tract? What would those look like?
- What colors would you use?
- Would you aim your tract at a specific audience or age-group, such as children, or teens, or people attending a particular event in the community?
- Would you make your tract seasonal or holiday-specific, or would you make a generic tract for use all year?

Group Suggestion: Have your Christian group, or smaller groups within the group, look at the various Gospel tracts the group leader has supplied. Ask each person, or a representative from each small group, to share his or her favorite tract and explain what they like about it.

Encourage the group to come up with a list of elements that every tract should include. Consider writing down this list on a board, or have each person write down the list on a piece of paper or in a personal notebook. The group leader could then explain that each person will be making his or her own tract at the next meeting. **OR** participants could draft their tracts at home during the week and bring their drafts to the next group meeting for discussion.

DAY 9

Draft Your Own Tract.

Enter HIS Gates With Thanksgiving.
Thank GOD for giving you the materials with which to design your own tract. Thank HIM that you live in modern times and have access to technologies like computers and the internet, which make such work easier than ever before. Thank GOD for the freedom of the press and for the those who fought to establish and preserve this freedom for you. Ask GOD for HIS wisdom in drafting a tract that will most effectively make JESUS known to every creature.

The Task
Design a rough draft of your own Gospel tract. Don't worry about images and format today. Just get the text down. You will have a chance to edit the tract tomorrow and add images later. This task should take you about 15 minutes, maybe a longer, depending on your style. Be sure to include the following basics of any Gospel presentation. I call these the 1-2-3 way to Heaven. I usually start my Gospel presentation with 2, then move to 1, then 3.

1 – There's 1 way to Heaven, 1 SAVIOR, 1 SON OF GOD, 1 MESSIAH. His name is JESUS and HE is GOD IN THE FLESH. HE created you. Only HE can recreate you.

2 – Every human has two problems that not a single one of us can solve—sin and death. We all sin, and as a consequence, we'll all die one day. If we die in our sin, we will experience eternal death in the Lake of Fire, known as Hell. Doing acts of charity and being kind cannot pay for sin or give us new, death-free bodies. Being a good person will never make you a new person. No human, saint, church leader, pope, angel, idol, or false god can forgive our sins. We need GOD HIMSELF to provide the solution to our sin and death. GOD sent HIS SON JESUS down from Heaven to Earth in the flesh to do just this.

3 – There are three things we must believe with all our heart to be saved—JESUS died, was buried, and rose on the third day. JESUS' death paid for our sins once and for all. His resurrection secures our resurrection. By HIS death, burial, and resurrection, sin and death are defeated, and all who believe can be made new—free from sin and death. Believers have the hope of their souls going to straight to Heaven when they die, and we also have the hope that JESUS will give us new, death-free bodies at the resurrection. We never have to worry about Hell.

Make sure to also include a statement about the consequences of rejecting JESUS. First, the person will remained trapped in sin, and sin only always gets worse, never better. Second, if the person dies without JESUS, HE or she will be cast into Hell for eternity. Define Hell as the Bible defines it—a place of eternal torment in the Lake of Fire. DO NOT define Hell as merely "separation" from GOD. Hell is more accurately a place of separation from GOD'S countenance or blessings. It is the place where HIS wrath and justice are poured out, without a drop of mercy or relief.

God created Hell to torment Satan and the fallen angels, so just imagine how awful it must be. We aren't doing anyone any favors by shielding them from the truth about Hell. God wishes none would perish in Hell, and HE gave up HIS own SON to give us a way out.

Group Suggestion: Have everyone draft a tract during meeting time or bring in a draft of a Gospel tract they created during the week. Then, have everyone buddy up and give feedback to each other. Perhaps each person could buddy up several times with a different partner each time so as to get a variety of feedback (kind of like speed dating).

Leave time at the end of the group meeting to talk about the kinds of edits each person will be making to his or her tract and why. Be on high alert for feedback that suggests participants should suppress the topics of sin and Hell. Christians should never subdue or edit GOD'S truths in order to make people more comfortable or to "itch the ears" of sinners who are offended by topics like sin and Hell. Just because a topic is unpopular in culture doesn't give Christians the liberty to exclude or modify it. JESUS commissions us to teach all that HE commands, not to edit HIS teachings according to cultural demands or personal preferences.

DAY 10
Make Your Tract Eye-catching.

Enter HIS Gates With Thanksgiving.
Thank GOD for the resources you will be using to edit your Gospel tract. Thank HIM for giving you an able mind and hands with which to do HIS work. Ask GOD to help you make the best decisions in the editing of your tract.

The Task
Refine the tract you drafted on Day 9. Now is the time to format the tract. Have fun experimenting with fonts and colors, adding pictures if you desire. Please make sure the images you use are not going to cause copyright issues.

When you're finished formatting, set your tract aside. A little time and some distance will help you to approach the tract with refreshed eyes for one last edit before you print it on Day 13. **Plan ahead:** If you don't have easy access to a printer, please plan ahead to go to a library or a place where you can print on Day 13. If you will be printing your tract at home, please make sure you have enough ink and paper, and if not, please go and get the supplies you will need for Day 13. You will also be printing a sign on Day 20, but you may find it easiest to do all your printing on one day.

Group Suggestion: Either have everyone format their tracts during meeting time, supplying lots of paper, markers, highlighters, and colored pencils, or have everyone format their tracts during the week and bring in their top design. Let each person present his top design to the group for feedback. If time permits, have everyone make edits and re-present their tracts.

For larger groups, consider having everyone work in smaller break out groups. If you desire, you can get fancy and use a projector or scan the tracts ahead of time and put them up on a screen for everyone to review together. Participants can also email their tracts to the leader before meeting time.

DAY 11
Plan a Visit and Prepare a Gift.

Enter HIS Gates With Thanksgiving.
Thank GOD for the resources you will be using in preparing a visit to your neighbor. Thank HIM that you live in a country where you can freely share your faith with others. Thank GOD for the men and women who have given their lives to afford you that freedom. **Pray** for GOD'S wisdom in planning a visit to a neighbor. **Pray** for your neighbor, that GOD will already be preparing his or her heart to receive JESUS. **Pray** for the faith and boldness to share the Gospel without shame.

The Task
Plan a visit to a neighbor you haven't met yet or haven't spoken to in a while. You will not actually visit your neighbor until Day 14, or on another day, if that works better for you. Select a Gospel tract you'd like to give your neighbor. It can be a tract from *Living Waters*, *EVANGELIZE GEORGIA*, or another source you prefer. You might also decide to give away one of your homemade tracts, which you will be printing on Day 13.

Buy or put together a small gift, such as a package of cookies, flowers from your yard (ideally, freshly picked on the day of your visit), or a handwritten note about how you're thinking about and praying for your neighbor. Set everything you have gathered aside until Day 14. Make sure to get a business card from your church or to collect any flyers about upcoming Christian events within the community to which you would like to invite this neighbor.

Plan on the day and time that you will be bringing your Gospel gift to this neighbor. Make sure to pick a time when the neighbor's car is present and when you most likely won't be interrupting a meal. You might even be able to catch your neighbor at the end of the workday when he is walking from his car to his house or getting his mail. You're not stalking but, rather, trying to be as considerate as possible with your timing.

Group Suggestion: Have group members take a minute to write down their plans for visiting a neighbor and their ideas for the gifts they might bring. Let each member share his plan with the group or a smaller break out group. The group leader(s) should offer useful feedback as needed.

DAY 12

Practice to Proclaim.

Enter HIS Gates With Thanksgiving.
Thank GOD for the gift of free speech and for the freedom of expression. Thank HIM that you live in a country where you can freely share the Gospel of JESUS CHRIST with others. Thank GOD for the *United States Constitution*, which protects our inalienable human right to free speech. Thank HIM for the lives sacrificed and for our current military, which helps to preserve our freedoms.

The Task
Practice explaining the Gospel to someone out loud, such as a friend, roommate, or family member. You can do this activity in front of a mirror if you don't have the opportunity to share with another person. Be sure your Gospel presentation includes the points you included in your tract, as explained in the evangelism task for Day 9.

After practicing your presentation, take a few minutes to think about the types of scenarios you might encounter when evangelizing in public. Ask yourself how you would respond to the following statements you might hear.
- I'm saved. I've been baptized.
- I'm a worship leader.
- I'm a member of such and such church.
- My grandma took me to church when I was younger.
- I'm Jewish, atheist, Muslim, Catholic…
- I'm searching, or I'm not sure what I think about GOD.

- God hates me because I'm gay.
- I believe in being kind to everyone and not judging others.
- I believe GOD will forgive anyone.
- I don't want to talk to you about JESUS.
- I'm uncomfortable with this conversation.
- You're harassing me.
- You should change your JESUS t-shirt.
- You should try a more creative approach to talking to people about GOD if you want them to listen.
- You're giving true Christians a bad name.
- I don't believe in being rude and talking to people about GOD.
- I'm trying to enjoy my evening with my family.
- I have peace with my beliefs, and I think everyone should find their own peace.
- GOD is good. That's all anyone needs to know.
- I'm glad you found faith. That's so good for you.
- My parents are Jehovah's Witnesses.
- My parents forced church on me, so I don't go anymore.
- I had bad experiences at church.
- People at church judged me.
- Churches should do something useful with their big buildings. Then, maybe people would be interested in GOD.
- No one has the right to tell others what to believe.
- No one can know for sure if GOD will accept them.
- Just be kind and good and you don't have to worry about GOD being angry at you.
- I've lived a good life. I raised my children and have been faithful to my job. I'm good.
- I'd rather go to Hell because my friends will be there.
- I think I've done enough charity to outweigh my sins.
- GOD understands. JESUS loves us. He wouldn't send anyone to Hell.
- Scaring people about Hell is manipulative.
- It's arrogant of GOD to tell people to worship HIM.
- I believe in science.
- The Bible was put together by men. How could it be GOD's word?
- The Bible is filled with contradictions and can't be trusted.
- The Bible has been translated too many times to be true.

- The Bible is filled with perverted ancient stories and has no value today.
- The Bible teaches bigotry and narrow-mindedness.

Some of these statements obviously reveal whether or not a person is in unbelief, but some unbelievers will make statements that sound almost Christian, or they will profess to be Christian. This is especially true of people trapped in cults, such as Mormons (LDS) and Jehovah's Witnesses. Never assume the person you are speaking with is saved, even if the person professes faith in JESUS and goes to church.

If a person makes Christian-sounding claims, probe more deeply. Ask him how he would explain to others how to get to Heaven. Even if the person is in church leadership, ask how he or she explains the Gospel to others. You might learn something, or you might discover that not everyone who professes JESUS truly knows HIM.

Bonus Task: Record a video of yourself giving a timed Gospel presentation. Play back the recording and make note of improvements you can make. Re-record the video until you're satisfied with your presentation. If you'd like, post one of the recordings online for others to view. All glory to GOD that you have the ability to proclaim the Gospel to anyone anywhere in the world, just by posting a video!!!

Group Suggestion: Take turns giving a short Gospel presentation in front of the group or smaller breakout groups. Try timing each other. See if you can get the whole message down to 2 minutes, then 1 minute, and then 30 seconds. Come up with several 5-second one liners you can say to someone in passing if you don't have time to stop for a full Gospel conversation.

Group leaders should give feedback and allow each participant to practice as many times as needed. Larger groups may want to break up into smaller groups or have members partner up so everyone gets a fair chance to work on their presentations. You may even want to dedicate 2-3 group meetings to this task.

Bonus: Have someone in the group record each Gospel presentation and make recordings available to all for critiquing and learning. **OR** have each group member submit a recording of his or her Gospel presentation before the group meeting. As a group or in small groups, watch each video presentation and give each other feedback.

Extra Bonus: At your meeting, have volunteers act out a Gospel conversation in pairs. You may ask a few brave souls do their act in front of the group. One person would play the role of evangelist and the other would be the person approached for a conversation. It might be best for the group leader to play the role of "the approached." Whoever plays this role should act out a variety of personas, such as the following:
- A professing "Christian" who thinks going to church gets you to Heaven
- A Catholic who believes being good and going to confession gets you to Heaven
- An atheist who believes in evolution. **Be informed:** Atheists will try to tell you they don't believe anything. That's a lie from Satan. Everyone believes in something.
- A hardened unbeliever who accuses evangelists of harassment
- An unbeliever who makes up an excuse about not having the time to talk
- A practicing witch, wizard, or Satanist
- A pleasant Pagan who is happy for you that you found "something that works" for your life
- An agonistic who is searching for answers
- A spiritual person who has found peace in her own way
- A Mormon or Jehovah's Witness
- A Muslim who thinks people choose their religion based on how they're raised
- A Hindu, New Age practitioner, Buddhist...
- A professing "Christian" who supports her homosexual friends
- A professing "Christian" who cross dresses
- A church leader who criticizes your Gospel knowledge and tells you to build relationships before witnessing to people
- A professing Christian who actually believes JESUS died on the cross for his sins

DAY 13

Edit and Print Your Tract.

Enter HIS Gates With Thanksgiving.
Thank GOD for the printer and ink you're using today. **Pray** that the printer will work well and that you will soon have a hardcopy of a Gospel tract that pleases GOD.

The Task
Read over your Gospel tract at least one more time and make any changes you need to make. Make sure you have the means to print or have gone to a location where you can print. Now, print your Gospel tract. If you like the way it looks, you're done for the day. If you're unsatisfied, then keep editing and reprinting until you have a satisfactory hardcopy. Even if you despise your own tract and would rather use one that someone else has created, please complete this task. Creating your own tract in an exercise that helps you to better understand how exactly to present the Gospel to others.

Bonus Task: If you'd like to print extra tracts to have on hand, then please do that. I suggest printing at least 5 extras if you would like to use your own tract for Days 14, 16 and 18-19. You might want to print 20+ tracts if you plan to do the bonus task for Day 21, which is to pass out tracts freely as you evangelize in public. And if you'd like to keep a tract for your own records, then please print one for that as well. **Personal Note:** I like to keep a folder with all my tracts—past, present, and future. It's basically my evangelism archive.

Plan Ahead: If you had to travel to get to a printer, then please also complete the task for Day 20, and print your FREE PRAYER sign, which is available on the *EVANGELIZE GEORGIA* website.

Group Suggestion: Have everyone bring in a final copy of their Gospel tracts to the group meeting. Seat the group in a circle and pass around each tract so everyone gets to see each one. Ask everyone to **pray** over the tracts as they circulate. For large groups, do this circle activity within smaller breakout groups.

DAY 14

Bless Your Neighbor With a Visit.

Enter HIS Gates With Thanksgiving.
Thank GOD for the Gospel gift you were able to put together for your neighbor on Day 11. Thank HIM for the opportunity to bless others and for a body that is able to do HIS Kingdom work. **Pray** that GOD gives you favor with your neighbor and that his or her entire household will receive the Gospel of JESUS CHRIST.

The Task
After carefully rereading the "Gospel Conversation Chart" in Chapter 2, take your Gospel gift to your neighbor and visit with him or her. If you have decided that today is not a good day, then please make your visit at a more opportune time. If your neighbor is unavailable, then keep trying to make your delivery until you have success, or make plans to visit a different neighbor. GOD might be shutting one door but opening another.

Pray the whole way to your neighbor's house. Be ready and willing to speak about spiritual things and to share the Gospel as the SPIRIT leads.

When you see your neighbor, introduce yourself and give her the gift you've prepared. Explain there's a church brochure with your gift. Ask your neighbor if she has a home church. If "yes," then you can say something like, "Would you say you have been reborn?" You'd be surprised to find that many churchgoers do not realize they must be reborn to enter GOD's Kingdom (**John 3:3**).

If the person says she doesn't go to church, try saying something like, "You don't have to be in church to know JESUS. Sometimes being in church helps." See how the person responds. Try following up with a question, such as "What's your spiritual upbringing?"

Remember, just because a person goes to church doesn't mean he or she is saved. And just because the person doesn't attend church doesn't mean he or she hasn't committed to JESUS. The topic of church is simply a springboard into the most important topic of all—the Gospel of JESUS CHRIST.

Once you have a feeling for the person's spiritual background, try saying something like, "The more important question is, are you committed to JESUS?" Continue to let the HOLY SPIRIT lead the conversation.

Before leaving, ask your neighbor if you can pray for her. Most people will accept prayer. Don't be discouraged if the person declines. A hardened unbeliever will be offended by each and every act of love you try to show her. Even the offer of prayer will be a stench to such a person.

If you encounter this kind of spiritual hardness, please understand the source of it is demonic. The "offended" person has been imprisoned by Satan and is in dire need of our prayers. **Pray** for this person, that he or she will humble herself before GOD and that Satan's blinding of her spiritual eyes will be undone so she can see the light of the Gospel (**2 Corinthians 4:3-4**). Thankfully, encounters like this are the exception in many locations, not the norm. However, there are locations where hardened unbelief is, sadly, the norm.

If the SPIRIT leads, ask your neighbor if she would like to join you at church or if she would like to exchange phone numbers for future contact. When the conversation has ended, politely dismiss yourself and **pray** for your neighbor all the way home.

Bonus Task: If the SPIRIT leads, you might ask your neighbor if he or she would like to pray to receive GOD's free gift of eternal life, right now. Please see the Gospel Conversation Chart in chapter 2 and the evangelism crash course (87 minutes long, 4 videos total) on the *EVANGELIZE GEORGIA* website for information on how to do that. I recommend having a copy of the "Rebirth Certificate" on you. You don't have to give the certificate away, but having a copy handy whenever you evangelize can help. The certificate can be printed out from the EVANGELIZE GEORGIA website.

Personal Note: Our family likes to deliver cookies and tracts to our immediate neighbors around Christmas time. I always give out store-bought cookies because I don't have time to bake cookies. With each delivery, I also include a church invite to a Christmas Eve service. I always ask if the neighbor attends church, and I take the opportunity to present the Gospel whenever possible. If the person has a home church, I will say something like, "The more important question is, are you ready for JESUS?" The conversation usually takes off from there.

Group Suggestion: Have everyone in your Christian group report back about their visits. Take a moment at the start of the meeting to get everyone to write down their thoughts. Then, ask each person to share. Break up lager groups into smaller ones, and have everyone share with his or her smaller group. **OR** complete the neighbor visits as a group, organizing everyone into pairs and sending two people to each house. Put a leader or a stronger speaker in each duo.

Personal Note: Whenever having group members share any experiences, it's best to get them to write down their thoughts ahead of time. At the start of your meeting, give everyone a few minutes and some paper and pens, and have them write down their thoughts. Then, have each person share. This keeps sharing time orderly, discourages one person from dominating the conversation, and encourages shy group members to say something.

DAY 15
Prayer Walk or Drive Among the Poor

Enter HIS Gates With Thanksgiving.
Thank GOD for your legs, your car, bike, wheelchair, or whatever means of transportation HE has given you. Thank HIM for the opportunity to intercede for your community. Thank HIM for the freedom to be able to walk around your community while praying in JESUS' name. Thank GOD for the men and women who fought to establish and preserve those freedoms. Thank GOD for giving you the privilege of ministering to the poor.

The Task

Drive through a poor neighborhood. Walk if you must, but please do not go at night and be careful. **Pray** for the salvation, deliverance, health, protection, and well-being of the people and businesses you see. Ask GOD to open doors and prepare hearts for the Gospel in these locations. Ask GOD to send you and others to proclaim the Gospel to the people and places HE desires.

Look for apartments and clusters of homes that would be good locations for evangelizing, Christmas caroling, reverse trick-or-treating, or blessing with door hangers. Reverse trick-or-treating is when you go door-to-door on Halloween, and instead of taking treats, you give away Bibles and tracts or a Gospel goodie bag to each household.

Bonus Task: As you walk around and pray, leave doorhangers on the doorknobs of the houses or apartments. You can order doorhanger bags online and fill them with tracts, little gifts, and church brochures, just like you would pack a Gospel goodie bag. Consider including seasonal candies and prizes if it's near a holiday. For example, around Resurrection Sunday, I like to hand out Easter eggs stuffed with QR codes to Gospel movies (in addition to a piece of candy). Salvation bracelets also make good egg stuffers. Always include an explanation of what the salvation colors mean with your bracelets. You can find instructions and literature about salvation bracelets on the *EVANGELIZE GEORGIA* website or through a *Google* search.

Extra Bonus Task: Paint salvation scriptures onto rocks and leave those in visible spots for people to find. Some verses to consider are **John 1:12, John 3:3, John 3:16-18, John 14:6, Acts 16:31, Romans 6:23, Romans 10:9, Romans 10:13. OR** print or write out these scriptures on paper and put them in Ziploc bags. Place the bags around to be found.

Group Suggestion: Do the prayer walk or drive with your Christian group. Break up larger groups into manageable teams and tackle different parts of a neighborhood or several different neighborhoods. Please be safe and wise. Do not go after dark. Reverse trick-or-treating might be one of the few exceptions of evangelizing after dark.

DAY 16

Make a Blessing Bag.

Enter HIS Gates With Thanksgiving.
Thank GOD for the materials with which you will be making your blessing bag. Thank HIM for the stores and employees that made the products available for purchase. Thank GOD for your hands and the ability to put together such a bag.

The Task
Make at least one quart-sized blessing bag to give to someone in need. A blessing bag is simply a bag with basic hygiene items and, of course, a Gospel tract. You can use one of your homemade tracts, one you bought, or one of the tracts from the *EVANGELIZE GEORGIA* website. Link and QR code given at the front of this book. Please see Chapter 4 for the checklist of items to include in your blessing bag. Please also see Chapter 4 for my comments on snack items and making a larger 1-gallon blessing bag. If you don't have time to make a blessing bag, then please see Chapter 4 for my suggestions for buying a meal gift card.

When making your bag, I suggest you include any church information, food pantry information, homeless shelter information, or brochures you think would be helpful. If it will fit inside the bag, you might also want to include a mini *New Testament* or *Gospel of John*. **Personal Note:** I have found that many homeless people have a Bible, or at least, they say they do.

When your blessing bag is complete, **pray** over it. Ask GOD to save, set free, and care after the person who receives it. **Pray** that the recipient would appreciate the items and not use them to barter for harmful substances. Ask GOD to protect you and give you HIS wisdom when you go to deliver the bag on Day 17, or on another day that you feel would be more opportune.

Group Assignment: Have the group make blessing bags together. The group leader can set out the items ahead of time. If the group is small, you can even go shopping for the items together. **OR** if you would rather have participants make their own bags, then the group leaders should send members home with a checklist at least two weeks beforehand. Have everyone bring in their blessing bags on an assigned day. The group leader could give away prizes for the most practical, most creative, or nicest looking bag.

This is also a great activity to get whole the church to help with. The congregation could supply the items on the checklist. Then, other groups within the church could assemble the bags, such as the women's ministry or youth. Even children can help in some way, either with packing the bags or selling crafts to raise money for the supplies.

OR Have your church or Christian group run a fundraiser to raise money for purchasing as many 10.00 McDonald's gift cards as you possibly can. One simple idea for raising funds would be to ask people not go out to dinner for a set number of weeks (maybe 2-4) and to donate what they would have otherwise spent.

You could also have a throw down between boys and girls or between smaller teams within the group. Each team could try to collect the most loose change from around their homes and from friends and family members. The winning team gets to pie the group leader in the face…or something like that.

DAY 17

Give Away Your Blessing Bag.

Enter HIS Gates With Thanksgiving.
Thank GOD for the transportation you will be using to make your blessing bag delivery. Thank HIM for the opportunity to be the hands and feet and mouth of CHRIST, delivering the Gospel of salvation and caring after someone in need. **Pray** that the HOLY SPIRIT guides you to someone who needs a blessing bag or gift card. **Pray** for good weather.

The Task
After carefully rereading the "Gospel Conversation Chart" in Chapter 2, drive or walk through the same poor areas of town you visited on Day

15, stopping when you see someone in need to whom you feel GOD is drawing you. Approach the person, introduce yourself, and explain that you have a blessing for him.

Offer the blessing bag or gift card. Explain that your gift is from your church and you're giving it in the name of JESUS. Even if you are not evangelizing with a church, you are the church. The blessing bag is a gift from the church universal, as in, Christians everywhere.

The person may or may not want the blessing bag. I kid you not, I have had homeless people reject blessing bags before. If the person rejects your blessing bag, you can always keep the unused blessing bag in your car for another day. Ask GOD to give you another opportunity to give the bag away. Whatever the person's response is to the bag, ask him if he has committed his life to JESUS, and ask how he would explain to someone else how to get to Heaven.

As the HOLY SPIRIT leads, present the Gospel. In your own words, explain to the person that GOD sent HIS SON JESUS to die on the cross for our sins. JESUS was buried and rose on the third day. Anyone who trusts in JESUS alone to make him fit for Heaven receives a clean soul and, at the resurrection, a new body that will never die. As a new creation in CHRIST, the believer will live with GOD forever in paradise. Those who reject JESUS will suffer eternal torment in Hell.

If the person wants to receive JESUS as SAVIOR, go over the "Certificate of Rebirth" if you have a copy (available on the *EVANGELIZE GEORGIA* website). Please see Days 14 and 21 for information how to lead someone in the sinner's prayer.

If you haven't already done so, ask for the person's name. Give your name in return. Then, ask if the person would like prayer for anything. **Pray** with the person. Then, ask the person if he has a Bible and supply one of your gift Bibles if needed. You may have already placed a gift Bible in the blessing bag.

Encourage the person to read the Gospel tract, study the Bible, and visit your church. Kindly dismiss yourself and depart from the person. When you get a chance, write down the person's name on your prayer list and **pray** over him or her regularly.

Personal Note: Many people I meet when evangelizing struggle with vision or reading issues. I like to include a QR code to a free audio Bible or Gospel movie in my tracts. I also like to have QR codes printed out for Gospel resources for Spanish and foreign language speakers. If I don't have codes on my tracts, I print out media codes on separate sheets of paper and include those in blessing bags and Gospel goodie bags. You can make your own QR codes for any media you'd like to include in your blessings bags by using a free QR code generator online, such as the one available at https://www.qr-code-generator.com/. **Caution:** Use discretion whenever including Christian media in your materials, and make sure not to create any copyright issues.

Bonus: You can also include QR codes to your own homemade Gospel presentation or Gospel media you might have posted online.

Group Suggestion: Have your Christian group or smaller break out groups deliver their blessing bags or meal cards together. Please use wisdom and exercise caution whenever evangelizing. As a rule, evangelize during daylight hours.

DAY 18

More Tracts!

Enter HIS Gates With Thanksgiving.
Thank GOD for the Gospel tracts HE provides. Thank HIM for all the materials HE supplies and for the opportunity to be a minister of the Gospel of JESUS CHRIST.

The Task
Print out three of the "FREE GIFT" tracts on the *EVANGELIZE GEORGIA* website, URL and QR code given at the front of this book. If you prefer to use the tract you've created, or a tract you have acquired from somewhere else, then please make sure you have three of those.

Pray over the tracts. Ask GOD to guide your tract distribution on Day 19.

Bonus: Put together three Gospel goodie bags with the tracts inside. Use a clear bags, such as sandwich bags or Ziplocs. Include small items such as candy, gum, ear plugs, stickers, a New Testament Bible or Gospel of John... If available to you, include a church business card or a brochure advertising an upcoming Bible study or Christian events going on in your community. Please see Chapter 4 for a checklist for Gospel Goodie bag items.

Group Suggestion: The group leader can print out the tracts ahead of time. If you so desire, the tracts can be printed on white paper or cardstock and group members can color and decorate them for fun. When the tracts or Gospel goodie bags are complete and ready for distribution, have the group **pray** over them.

DAY 19

Bless Three Strangers.

Enter HIS Gates With Thanksgiving.
Thank GOD for the abundance of restaurants and businesses in your town. Thank HIM for the abundance of opportunities to bless people and employees everywhere with the Gospel message. **Pray** that you find favor with those to whom you give Gospel tracts or goodies.

The Task
Give away the three tracts or goodie bags you've prepared to complete strangers. A simple way to do that is to walk into a fast food restaurant and hand the goodies to the person behind the counter. Explain that you appreciate all the employees do and wanted to leave a blessing for the employees working that day. **Personal note:** Oftentimes I will say the blessing is from my church, especially if I have included a church brochure in the bags. Again, you can say the tract or goodie bag is from your church, even if it's from you personally because you are the church.

Another suggestion for handing out the tracts or goodie bags is to hand one to a cashier or barista who took care of you that day. As you hand the tract to the person, say something kind like, "Thank you for taking care of me today. Here's a gift of appreciation."

You can also leave a tract or goodie bag for your server at a restaurant along with a generous tip. On your way in and out of the restaurant, give out the other tracts to servers, bartenders, hostesses, or busboys. Never leave a tract in lieu of a tip.

Bonus or Alternative Task: Give your tracts to neighbors you meet while out and about or hang tracts or goodie bags from doorknobs. Do not, however, put anything on or inside mailboxes. Tampering with mailboxes is a Federal offense. Doorhangers are generally legal. If you don't have doorhanger bags, you can make your own by attaching a string or ribbon to your Gospel goodie bag, or knotting the bag in such a way that it can hang from a doorknob.

Group Suggestion: Deliver your tracts or Gospel goodie bags as a group by breaking everyone up into pairs. Have everyone report back about their experiences at the end of your meeting time or at the next meeting. **OR** ask everyone to deliver their Goodie bags during the week and report back at the next meeting. As always, at the start of the meeting, give everyone time to write down their thoughts. When sharing experiences, make sure each person gets a fair chance to speak.

Personal Note: Although people are generally happy to receive Gospel goodie bags, you will occasionally meet people who throw away or destroy Gospel tracts. Most people will wait until you're out of sight before committing their crime, but some people will destroy, throw away, or toss aside your tracts right in front of your face. Do not be taken by surprise. JESUS warned us things like this would happen when we minister in HIS name.

If I see someone throw away a tract, I will fish it out of the garbage in front of them. Sometimes, the culprit will show shame and apologize for having tossed the tract. The HOLY SPIRIT works to convict the world of sin and the need for JESUS. Unashamedly fishing tracts out of the garbage is one way we can work alongside this conviction. If nothing else, the action communicates to those who watch that the Gospel message is worth pulling from the trash.

The HOLY SPIRIT will be grieved whenever the Gospel message is mistreated, and as a result, you will most likely feel upset when you encounter people who reject, destroy, or discard your materials. It's the Christian reaction to be grieved when you meet a person so deceived by Satan that he or she treats the Gospel of salvation with disdain. **Pray** hard for this person. Put the person on your prayer list, even if you don't have a name for him. GOD knows who you mean when you pray for "the young man who threw my tracts on the floor at the food court."

DAY 20

Print Your Sign and Pray.

Enter HIS Gates With Thanksgiving.
Thank GOD for the resources you'll be using to make or print an evangelism sign. Thank HIM that you live in a country where you can proclaim the Gospel freely in public forums. Thank GOD for the *United States Constitution* and for the people who have sacrificed so much to establish and maintain our freedoms. **Pray** that your sign will glorify GOD and point people to JESUS. Ask GOD for good weather for Day 21.

The Task
Either make or print out a sign that says FREE PRAYER or NEED PRAYER? You may design your own sign, or print the FREE PRAYER sign from the *EVANGELIZE GEORGIA* website, URL and QR code given at the front of this book. I like to print my signs on standard computer paper or cardstock (8.5X11 inches). Feel free to make your sign larger if you have the means. Use brightly colored paper or cardstock for best results. Protect your sign from the elements by placing it inside of a laminate folder or plastic sleeve. You can even use a large Ziploc bag or cellophane wrap and tape in a pinch.

If you handwrite your sign, you can use standard-sized paper, or you can get fancy and use poster board. Make sure your writing is clear and bold. For lettering, you can use poster paint or simply go over each letter with a sharpie several times. Use stencils if you like. When you have your sign, **pray** GOD gives you HIS wisdom about where to go with it on Day 21.

Bonus: Attach your FREE PRAYER sign to the back of a clipboard. Use the clipboard to write down names and phone numbers for following up with the people you speak with to Day 21. Tape a copy of the rebirth certificate and sinner's prayer onto your clipboard for reference. The certificate is available on the *EVANGELIZE GEROGIA* website, the link and QR code for which can be found at the start of this book. **Personal note:** I also like to tape a copy of the spiritual inventory questions from the *Great Exchange* onto my clipboard. These questions are great for getting Gospel conversations going. The *Great Exchange* surveys can be found here: https://thegreatexchange.org/resources/

Group Suggestion: Create or color your signs as a group. Maybe have the group leader or a panel of judges pick the top signs. Give away prizes for categories like boldest colors, most creative, neatest handwriting… **Pray** over the completed signs together.

DAY 21
Evangelize in Public.

Enter HIS Gates With Thanksgiving
Thank GOD for the day. Thank HIM for the public places around your town. Thank GOD for using you to minister the GOSPEL of JESUS CHRIST. Thank the HOLY SPIRIT for all HE has taught you and will continue to teach you as you proclaim the Gospel to others. Ask GOD to guide your steps, protect you, and lead you to the people who are seeking and in need of JESUS. Thank JESUS for being with us always, even unto the End of the Age.

The Task

After carefully rereading the "Gospel Conversation Chart" in Chapter 2, take your FREE PRAYER sign to a busy public location, such as a park or high-traffic sidewalk and stand or walk around while holding it. As a US citizen, you are free to engage in public speech at any public forum, which includes public parks, sidewalks, and streets.

If you are a tax paying citizen of any US state, you are free to walk around and enjoy any public campus in the United States. As a rule, it's best to keep away from dorms and the student center. Evangelizing or preaching outside of classrooms could also cause disturbances and issues for you. Dining halls (other than the student center), outside of libraries, and other popular spots on campus are generally fine for visitors to frequent and engage in conversations with students. Colleges might try to limit your activities to the "free speech" zone. Free speech zones are unconstitutional, but that's just the way things are these days. Technically, the whole campus is a free speech zone, especially for students and secondarily for tax payers (at least most sidewalks and amenities).

Some states, such as Georgia at the moment, recognize how wrong it is to limit free speech to a zone on public campuses. GOD bless Governor Brian Kemp for signing legislation that bans schools from creating free speech zones! Sadly, other states will trample on basic human rights without a second thought. We must all **pray** for and exercise our rights if we want to keep them.

Private campuses have different rules, so be aware of those if you go to a private campus. Even then, what's to stop you from touring the campus and praying with the students you meet along the way and blessing them with Gospel goodies? And you can always evangelize at busy sidewalks and hangout spots surrounding any given campus. Whatever it is you do, always proceed with prayer and wisdom.

College professors have less rights to speak openly in the classroom on public college campuses because they are government workers and subject to the laws that separate church and state. Even so, professors can incorporate the Bible into appropriate lessons. For example, there's no rule against comparing and contrasting the flood of *Gilgamesh* with the flood of Noah, and such comparisons can only enrich the students' education. Also, a professor can help oversee Christian clubs and Bibles studies on campus and serve as a light and an encouragement to the Christian students. As always, ask GOD for HIS wisdom in matters like this—and all other matters.

Bonus: If you would like to host an official evangelism or preaching event at a public college, you will most likely need to email the Dean of Students with your request. Make sure to include your desired location. (If the free speech zone is in a good spot, that might be best.) Also, include details, such as the day and time of your visit, the expected number of people at the event, what church or organization you are with, the nature of the event, and any other information the college will need. It might take months to get a reservation or permit for your event, so pack your patience. **Personal Note:** I like to set up a Prayer Tent (or table) for students during midterms and finals. I like Tuesdays and Wednesdays from 11AM-1PM, with setup at 10AM and breakdown by 2PM. At these events, our evangelism team prays with students, shares the Gospel, and hands out stress relief goodie bags. The goodie bags contain Gospel tracts and fun items like a #2 pencil and snacks.

If you don't live near a campus or busy city center, you might have better odds at engaging with others in a grocery store parking lot. Parking lots are considered private property, not public forums, so if you do go to a parking lot, keep moving through it until you see someone who looks interested in your sign. Stop and have a natural conversation with that person. You will most likely not be accused of anything suspicious if you're simply engaging in a private conversation in a parking lot. I can't speak for all parking lots, so please ask GOD for HIS wisdom. You might also have success in parking lots by going around without a sign and simply approaching people who are sitting on a bench or at a table. Such folks are usually on a break or have time to talk. I've had many fruitful conversations this way.

As you walk around in public with your FREE PRAYER sign, notice how the people around you respond. Some will rush away. Others might mock you. Some will smile politely as they pass by, and others will eagerly engage in conversation with you. Try to have at least one conversation with someone who seems responsive to your sign (or approach).

Introduce yourself to the person and explain you're offering FREE PRAYER. Then, ask this person how you can pray for him or her. Explain that when you pray, you pray in JESUS' name. Ask the person if she has committed to JESUS. If "yes," then ask her to explain how to get to Heaven. If "no," then explain the Gospel of JESUS CHRIST.

If the person has not received JESUS yet, then ask if he or she would like to receive HIM right now. If yes, then Praise GOD! Go over the rebirth certificate (if you completed the bonus assignment for Day 20) and then **pray** with the person to receive JESUS. You may use the Sinner's Prayer or **pray** in your own words. Please watch the 87-minute (4-video) Evangelism Crash Course on the *EVANGELIZE GERORGIA* website for more information on how to pray with a person who wants to commit to JESUS.

No worries if you don't have the rebirth certificate or Sinner's Prayer memorized. You can simply explain to the person what it means to accept JESUS as SAVIOR and LORD and **pray** for the person to receive salvation. Make sure to also **pray** for the person over his or her specific prayer request. **Encourage the new believer to pray** to GOD in his or her own words when you have finished praying. Leave a moment of silence for this. The person may or may not pray. As the HOLY SPIRIT leads, have the person repeat the prayer below, or a similar prayer, after you. Break down the sentences into very short phrases for best results. I have emboldened every other phrase to illustrate where to possibly break up the phrases.

HOLY FATHER, I am a sinner. **I can't save myself.** I believe YOUR SON JESUS **died on the cross** as payment for my sins. **HE was buried** and rose on the third day. **I believe JESUS CHRIST** is GOD IN FLESH. **JESUS, please be my SAVIOR** and LORD. **YOU are my only hope for Heaven.** Please seal and baptize me **with the HOLY SPIRIT.** I can't wait for the day **when I will be resurrected** into an immortal body **like YOURS.** I give up all false beliefs **and sin.** I will live by faith in you. **Thank you JESUS** for your blood. **It's in your name** I pray. **Amen.**

When the prayer has ended, encourage the person to come to your church, or to go to a local church, and get baptized. If you haven't done so already, write down the person's name and prayer request on your clipboard so you can **continue to pray** over him or her during the week. Ask if the person would like someone from your church or Christians group to reach out to him or her. If yes, get the person's phone number

If the person does not want to receive JESUS, ask for the reason for this hesitation. Lovingly explain the consequences of rejecting JESUS and explain we are not guaranteed our next breath. **Personal Note:** Sometimes, if a person is hesitant to receive JESUS, **I will pray** with her, that she will be unblinded and see the light of the Gospel. Some people have accepted JESUS after praying this kind of prayer. All glory to GOD! Let the HOLY SPIRIT guide your steps.

BONUS: Have tracts or Gospel goodie bags on you, ready to hand out to those who stop and talk with you. Or hand out tracts freely as you walk around in search of someone with whom to engage in conversation. When I go on an evangelism outing like this, I like to have 50-100 business card tracts on me, more if I know I'm going to a busy location or event.

Group Suggestion: Go to a busy public park, public street fair or public location where people spend a lot of leisure time. Split up into pairs, or small groups, and have each pair complete the task together. I highly recommend that group leaders engage in the first few conversations while the group members observe the conversations. Then, send out group members to go and do likewise. I also suggest evangelizing in pairs if possible. Please be wise and safe.

Extra Bonus Task or an Alternative For Those Who Can't Go Out in Public: If you have trouble getting out, or you would like to add another avenue of reaching others with the Gospel, consider starting a prayer hotline, prayer email account, video chat, or something like that. As of the time I'm writing this book, you can get a free *Google* phone number and make business cards or car magnets advertising FREE PRAYER with the phone number or email address or website on it. You could simply advertise the hotline number or "prayer request" email address on your *Facebook* page, or whatever social media you use, or you could make *YouTube* videos advertising the number or email address. Post these videos online and invite viewers to contact you. If your church has an electronic sign, consider advertising your hotline number or email address there.

If you set up a phone line, I suggest making a recording that tells people to hang up and call 9-11 if they are having an emergency or thoughts about ending their life. I would also include a Gospel message in the recording so people can hear that if they are waiting on hold.

If you opt for email prayer requests, I suggest setting up a separate email account and having an automated response that lets senders know the message has been received and that you will **pray** over it, and on what date. I would also include a Gospel explanation in this automated message.

If you post videos online, you could simply ask people to leave prayer requests in the comments section. Make sure to share the Gospel in your videos, and maybe explain to viewers how and when you **pray** over the requests. For example, let them know you pray over a column of requests each day and that each person gets prayed over once per month, or something like that.

You can keep your prayer hotline or email limited to local requests, depending on how you advertise, or you can cast a wider net and advertise broadly. If you do that, I suggest asking more people to join you in praying over the requests. Are there some homebound prayer warriors in your church who can join you? Or, if the SPIRIT leads, your entire church could undertake a prayer hotline ministry. **Personal Note:** I am in favor of live phone calls and conversations, as opposed to asynchronous communications, such as emails, comments, and prayer boxes. When you communicate live, you have a great opportunity to share the Gospel and mister personally, but asynchronous communications certainly have their place.

MY PARTING WORDS TO YOU

This concludes our 21 days of evangelism. Please don't stop. Keep at it. Repeat the tasks in this book, or pick your favorites and do them frequently. Have a goal to give away a tract or share the Gospel with at least one person every day. Plan to go evangelizing in public regularly, such as once a month, once every two weeks, or once a week.

As you become more comfortable going with the Gospel, try casting a wider net. Go to public city events with Christian friends. Try registering an evangelism booth at a city event with your church or Christian group. **Personal Note:** At city street fairs, I like to host a game booth where I play a JESUS trivia spin-the-wheel game with participants. Church friends are more likely to get on board for events like this than they are for plain and simple on-foot evangelism.

Never underestimate the power of GOD and the efficacy of on-foot evangelism. In other countries, our Brothers and Sisters may have nothing but a Bible. Many of them don't even have that. And yet, they will be faithful to JESUS' command, going and evangelizing entire territories on-foot, planting hundreds of churches along the way. Our FATHER will care for you however and wherever you go with the Gospel of HIS SON.

> The LORD bless you, and keep you;
> The LORD make His face shine on you,
> And be gracious to you;
> The LORD lift up His countenance on you,
> And give you peace. -**Numbers 6:24-26**

Alicia Tubbs is an evangelist for her SAVIOR and LORD JESUS CHRIST, the wife of the best husband ever, a homeschool mom of two big little blessings, and a homesteader. She can be found online at evangelizegeorgia.org.

Made in United States
Orlando, FL
21 June 2024